100
essential
embroidery
stitches

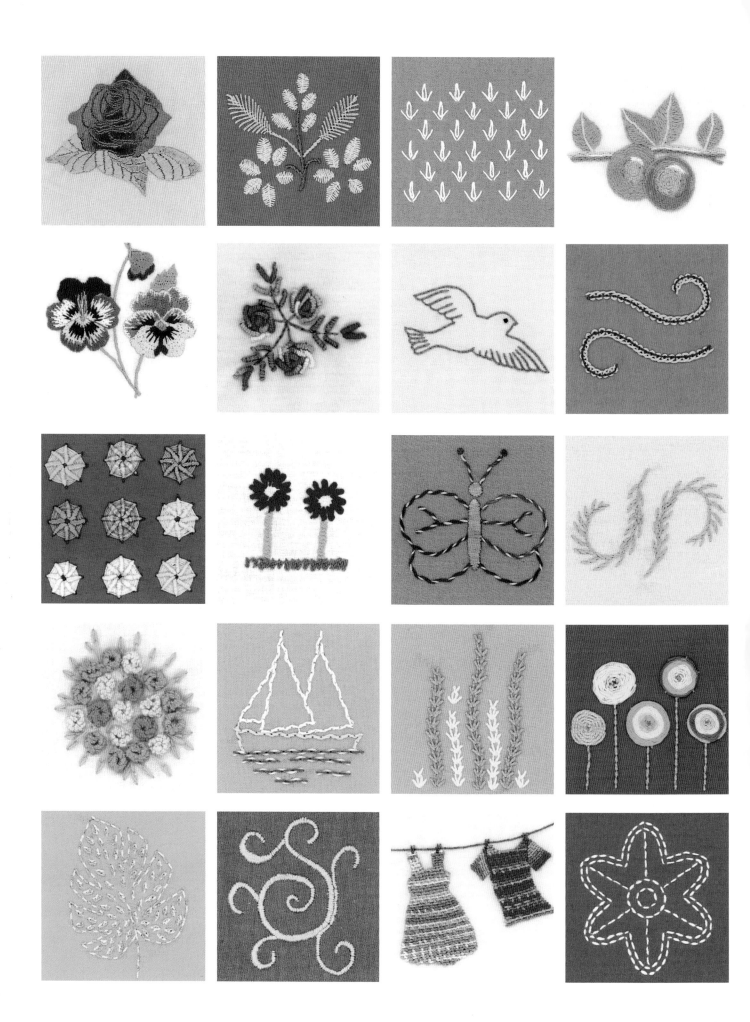

100
essential
embroidery
stitches

SUSIE JOHNS

THE GUILD OF MASTER CRAFTSMAN PUBLICATIONS

Contents

Lines and Outlines

Bands and Borders

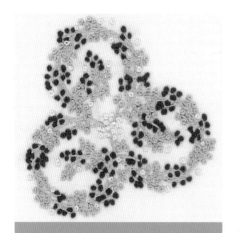

Isolated Stitches and Motifs

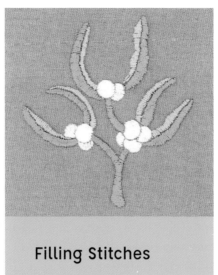

Filling Stitches

Couching and Laid Work

Introduction

The embroidery in this book is like 'painting' with thread. This kind of embroidery, on plain-weave fabric, is known as surface embroidery, or 'freestyle'. Most of the stitches are worked without much regard to the weave of the fabric and, unlike other related embroidery techniques such as canvaswork, blackwork, hardanger and counted cross stitch, stitches can be large or small, made in any direction and using a wide range of different threads and yarns.

Some stitches – mostly those that form narrow lines – are used for outlining, while wider stitches can be used as decorative bands or frames. Others are used for filling and making textures, patterns and various interesting effects.

With this in mind, this book is divided into five sections, grouping together the different kinds of stitches – though some of the more versatile stitches deserve to be included in more than one section. Most of the outline stitches, for example, can be worked in close rows as a solid filling; while many isolated stitches can be repeated and scattered within a shape, as an open or closed filling, depending on the spacing, or repeated in rows to create a border.

Once you have mastered the most basic stitches, you can add a few more unusual and challenging ones. Practise them on scraps of fabric or make a stitch sampler: a piece of fabric on which you embroider examples of the various stitches – as many or as few as you like – as a reference.

You will now be ready to use these stitches to create decorative embroideries. Draw the outline of your design on a piece of fabric, choose a palette of coloured threads, and start stitching.

Difficulty ratings for stitches

Each stitch is rated from one to three, to denote degrees of difficulty. Those rated one are easy enough for a beginner; those rated two start to get a bit trickier, requiring some expertise; and three is reserved for the most difficult of stitches. None, however, is that difficult, especially if you follow the illustrated step-by-step instructions – and remember that practice makes perfect!

Tools and Materials

Embroidery, compared to many other crafts, requires little in the way of basic equipment: you simply need a needle, fabric and thread to get started. In addition to these essentials, a few other items will help you produce better results. This section gives an overview of everything you'll need.

Fabric

For surface embroidery, you will need a plain-weave fabric. Cotton or linen are the best choices, with a smooth, tightly woven texture. Both cotton, which is relatively inexpensive, and linen, which costs a little more, are natural fabrics: the reason for choosing these is that the needle glides in and out more easily than it does with synthetics. To prove this for yourself, try out some sample stitches on a piece of pure cotton or linen and then try some on a poly-cotton or other synthetic fabric.

For everyday items such as tablecloths and bedlinen, which need to be washed fairly frequently, you need to use a practical fabric such as cotton or linen. If you are making a picture, panel or wallhanging, however, you can be more experimental with your fabric choices. Whatever you choose, it is still a good idea to try out a few stitches on some offcuts or scraps, to make sure that the fabric suits your stitching technique.

Linen

Cotton twill

Fine cotton

Preparing fabric

When using natural fabrics, if they are not pre-shrunk, they should be washed and ironed before you begin stitching. This applies even if the finished item is something like a framed picture, which will not be laundered, as washing the fabric makes it softer and easier to work with, allowing the needle to glide through easily.

TIP Keep a bag of fabric scraps to hand. However small, you never know when these might come in handy as test swatches or to embellish a stitched motif.

Thread

Thread is a vital component: after all, it is the material from which the stitches are formed. Try to use the best threads you can afford as cheaper versions can be rather inferior in quality, with a tendency to break, and the dyes might run when the embroidered fabric is washed. There are various types of thread available.

1 Six-stranded cotton embroidery thread, known in the US as floss, is very versatile and probably the most popular of all the embroidery threads. Loosely wound in a skein, individual threads can be separated and then combined, so you can use any number of threads. The number of strands should suit the scale of the design and the weight of the fabric.

2 Satin embroidery thread, sometimes referred to as satin floss, is another stranded thread, usually made from rayon (viscose) or from silk.

3 Coton à broder is a smooth, twisted thread made from four non-divisible strands and is finer than perle, making it suitable for delicate stitching.

4 Soft cotton is a thick cotton yarn with a matt appearance; more usually suited to needlepoint, it can be used in freestyle embroidery when working on coarsely woven fabrics, and as a couching thread.

5 Perle thread is a non-divisible thread with a characteristic twisted appearance. It is sold in twisted skeins and in balls. This thread is available is four thicknesses: #3, #5, #8 and #12. Size #3 perle cotton approximately equates to six strands of embroidery floss, and size #12 is the finest and arguably the most suitable for surface embroidery.

Other threads, made from different fibres such as wool, silk, linen and metal, are also available but have not been used in this book.

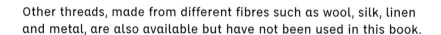

TIP Look after your embroidery threads. They may look attractive arranged in an open basket but if left for too long they can tangle, become discoloured, dirty or even fade (though good-quality threads are more light-fast than cheaper ones). It is a good idea to store unused threads in a container with a lid. You can buy special thread storage boxes, though a shoe box will do the job just as well. You may prefer to sort threads into colours or types and store them in zip-lock plastic bags.

Scissors

Embroidery scissors are small with sharp, pointed blades, essential for snipping threads and cutting away small areas of fabric. For cutting out fabric pieces, you will need a larger pair of scissors which should be reserved for cutting only fabric – never paper – and a pair of all-purpose scissors for cutting paper and card when making templates. Scissors should be kept sharp: blunt scissors will make cutting fabric difficult. Pinking shears are useful for cutting fabrics that are liable to fray.

Pinking shears.

Needles

It is essential to have the right needle for the task. You need to choose a needle that is suitable for the thickness of the fabric and the thread.

Crewel needles are designed for embroidery. They are medium-length with a sharp point and a long eye to accommodate several thicknesses of thread. The longer eye makes them easier to thread. They are available in sizes 1 to 12: the smaller the number, the finer the needle. Try to use the smallest possible needle, as it will be easier to push through the fabric. Your choice will be influenced by the number of thread strands you are using. As a guideline, a size 4 or 5 will accommodate two strands of stranded cotton; for three strands you will need a size 6 or 7.

Chenille needles also have a long eye and are typically longer and thicker than crewel needles; they come in sizes 14 to 26. They are useful for doing embroidery on heavier fabrics and with thicker threads.

Tapestry needles (also in sizes 14 to 26) are typically thicker, with a long eye and a blunt tip and are used for whipping and weaving between threads where it is important not to split threads or pierce the fabric.

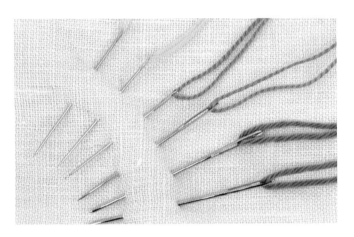

From left to right: crewel needles, chenille needles and tapestry needles.

Changing needles

After a lot of use, a needle will become blunt, so if you are finding it difficult to push a needle through the fabric, or if the fabric snags when you push the needle through, discard it and use a new one.

Embroidery hoops

These consist of two wooden or plastic rings, the larger of which has a screw that can be tightened or loosened to accommodate fabrics of different weights. Most are round, though novelty shapes that are slightly more triangular, square, oval or hexagonal are also available. Hoops hold the fabric taut, which is important when working stitches that might otherwise cause the fabric to pucker and distort.

As a general rule, stretching fabric in an embroidery hoop makes it easier to control the embroidery stitches and achieve an even tension. You can adjust each stitch as it is formed, making sure that it sits neatly on the surface of the fabric: without a hoop, there can be a tendency for the thread to be pulled too tightly and the fabric to become puckered.

Hoops are available in a range of sizes from about 7cm (3in) to 30cm (12in) in diameter. Most people find a relatively small hoop of about 12–20cm (5–8in) easiest to work with. Bear in mind that the hoop can be moved around your piece of work, so there is no need to buy a hoop that is larger than your project.

Other useful items

Dressmakers' pins can be useful for holding layers of fabric together or for holding threads and ribbons in place when couching. Buy good-quality steel pins that will not rust or become blunt; keep them in a lidded box.

A tape measure is useful for measuring fabric, while a ruler is invaluable for drawing straight lines accurately.

A thimble is a useful accessory for some sewers, while others find it unnecessary or cumbersome.

Markers

With most hand embroidery, you will need to mark guidelines on the fabric so that you know where to place the stitches. If the stitches will cover these lines completely – as in satin stitch, for example – the lines can be drawn with some kind of permanent marker. If, however, the stitches will be more open and the design lines will show through, then the lines need to be drawn with a marker that will fade or that can be removed. Some pens and pencils are suitable for making marks directly on the fabric and some are used to transfer marks from paper to fabric using a heat source such as an iron.

For drawing permanent lines, a ballpoint pen (not a gel pen or rollerball) or an ordinary graphite pencil can be used. Before using one on a project, however, do a test to make sure the marks are permanent. Draw some marks on a scrap of fabric using your pen or pencil, then dampen the fabric and rub the marks with your fingertips, to make sure they do not smudge or run.

For making temporary marks on fabric, there are various pens and pencils available. The ones that fade away by themselves are most useful for small areas of embroidery that are to be finished quite quickly, as you don't want the marks to fade before you have had a chance to finish the stitching.

Lines drawn with water-erasable markers will last longer and can be removed with water once the embroidery is complete. For small areas, to remove the pen marks, try rubbing them with a cotton bud dampened with cold water; for larger areas, you may need to immerse the fabric in water in order to remove the marks. Once again, it is wise to practise on a scrap of fabric first.

Tailors' chalk pencils, some of which have a brush on the end for erasing chalk marks, are useful for marking designs on dark fabrics. Transfer pens and pencils leave permanent marks on fabric.

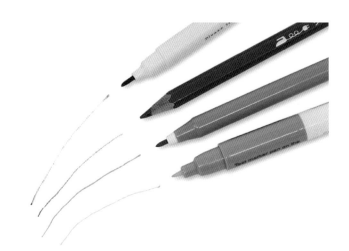

Erasable markers and a chalk pencil.

TIP **Always try out markers on a spare scrap of fabric. Draw a few lines, leave for a while, then wash with cool water. Some pens create marks that are difficult to erase and you don't want to complete a piece of embroidery before discovering that the marked lines of your design cannot be removed.**

Iron

A steam iron is invaluable for embroidery work. When pressing an embroidered piece, you should avoid squashing and flattening the stitches. To do this, place a folded towel underneath to provide a cushioned bed for the embroidery, place the embroidery right side down and cover it with a pressing cloth before ironing carefully.

Preparing to Stitch

When working embroidery stitches on a plain-weave fabric, it is important to match the weight of the thread and the thickness of the needle to the fabric. If the needle is too thick, it is likely to create holes in the fabric and if the thread is too thick, it will not sit neatly on the surface of the fabric.

Marking designs

Direct tracing is the easiest, quickest and most straightforward way of drawing a design on fabric. A lightweight fabric may be thin enough to lay on top of a design in order to trace the lines directly. With fabrics that are less translucent, you will find a light box useful, to make the lines of the design visible through the fabric. These days, light boxes are much smaller and more portable than they used to be. Instead of a cumbersome frame involving light bulbs, wires and bulky plugs, modern LED light boxes are really slim – about the size of an A4 sketchbook – and with USB connections. If you don't have a light box, however, you can improvise by taping the design to a window: tape the fabric on top and you should be able to see the design and trace it onto the fabric. With any direct tracing method, you will usually first need to trace or photocopy the design onto plain paper.

An alternative to tracing is to make a heat transfer. For this, you will need a heat transfer pen or pencil – available from embroidery suppliers – and thin white paper, such as lay-out or 'bank' paper (but not tracing paper, which tends to cockle under the heat of the iron). Lay the paper over the design and trace it, using the special transfer pen or pencil. Then lay your fabric on an ironing board, lay the tracing face down on the fabric and carefully press with a hot iron, taking care that the paper's position doesn't shift or the transferred lines will be blurred. After the allotted time – and you should check the guidelines for your particular pen or pencil – you can lift off the paper to reveal the design on the fabric. One thing to bear in mind here: when using this method, your design will be reversed, so reverse your chosen motif or lettering when making your initial drawing.

Enlarging and reducing motifs

If you find a motif you would like to embroider but want it to be larger or smaller, you can easily change the size by scanning the motif on to a computer and altering the scale, or by using the reducing and enlarging facility on a photocopier. To work out exactly how to achieve a particular size, there are formulas for calculating the percentage.

To enlarge a motif
Measure the motif you wish to use, decide what size you want it to be, divide the desired size by the original size, then multiply by 100 to achieve the percentage.
For example, if the original motif is 5cm (2in) high and the desired size is 12.5 cm (5in) high:
$12.5 \div 5 = 2.5 \times 100 = 250$
You will need to photocopy the motif at 250%.

To reduce a motif
This is done in the same way as enlarging but the numbers will be different and you will expect the calculated percentage to be less than 100.
For example, if the original motif is 5in (12.5cm) high and the desired size is 2in (5cm) high:
$5 \div 12.5 = 0.4 \times 100 = 40$
You will need to photocopy the motif at 40%.

An ordinary ballpoint pen is suitable for drawing permanent lines on fabric.

TIP **Choose your marker according to your fabric and the stitches you intend to use. Some stitches will completely cover all marked design lines, so it will not matter if the marks are permanent. Some stitches will not cover the lines, however, and the marks will need to be erased.**

Preparing the fabric

Your fabric should be smooth and wrinkle free, so press it with a hot iron before stitching to remove creases.

Choose an embroidery hoop smaller than your piece of fabric. You will discover with practice what size of hoop feels most comfortable and practical for you. You may wish to see the whole design within the hoop or you may prefer to use a small hoop and move it to different areas of the design as you work. So that the fabric is held firmly between the rings of the hoop, it is a good idea to bind the inner ring using cotton tape, bias binding or bias-cut strips of fabric.

Place your fabric on top of the plain ring of the embroidery hoop, then place the other part of the hoop – the one with the opening and the screw fitting – on top, pressing it down until the two parts of the ring align. You may have to loosen the screw in order for it to fit and, once in place, you will need to tighten the screw so that the fabric is firmly held in place. Tug gently on the edges of the fabric so that it is nice and taut – but take care not to distort the fabric, as the grain should be kept straight.

The cut edges of the fabric are liable to fray, so you may wish to hem them or simply trim them with pinking shears.

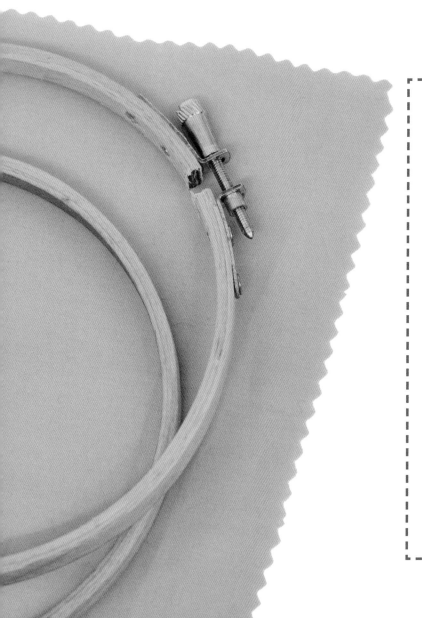

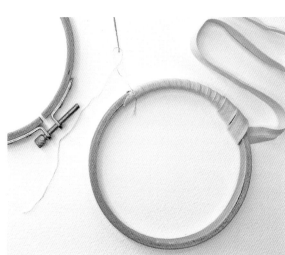

Binding a hoop

Wrap one end of the strip around the hoop and fasten with a few stitches. Wind the strip around in a diagonal fashion until you reach the starting point, then attach the end with a few more stitches.

Preparing the thread

Six-stranded embroidery thread is sold in skeins, held in place with two paper bands. Do not remove these bands but hold the skein in one hand and pull on the loose end to draw out a length of thread. Separate this length into the number of strands you wish to use – typically, one, two or three strands. Separate the strands by pulling them out individually. If you try to pull out more than one at a time, they will most likely tangle and knot together.

If your skein does become tangled, you may wish to wind the thread onto a bobbin. These are sold precisely for this purpose and are available made from card or plastic. You can keep a record of the thread shade number by writing it on the bobbin and bobbins can be stored in a box with a lid to keep them organised and dust free.

When using perle thread from a ball, simply cut the length you require. Twisted skeins are slightly more tricky to handle: I suggest that you remove the paper labels, untwist the skein and lay it flat, then open out one end to create a loop. Cut the skein once to produce lengths of thread each measuring about 90cm (36in). Knot the cut ends at both ends, then retwist them into a skein for storage. A single length of thread can be removed from the skein by untwisting and cutting both ends of the strand.

Threading a needle

Sometimes it can be difficult to pass the cut ends of embroidery thread through the eye of a needle, especially if you are using more than one strand. One solution is to fold the ends of the threads over the needle, pull tight, then pass the fold through the eye, instead of the cut ends themselves. Another solution is to use a needle threader or, if you haven't got one, a small strip of folded paper.

A needle threader has a wire loop that you push through the eye of the needle; pass the end of the thread through the loop, then withdraw the wire loop from the needle, thereby pulling the thread through the eye. If you haven't got a needle threader, you can improvise with a short length of very thin wire.

A good alternative is to use a small strip of thin paper folded in half. Cut a piece of paper about 5cm (2in) long and narrower than the eye of the needle, fold it in half across its width, place the end of the thread inside the fold and push the fold through the eye of the needle.

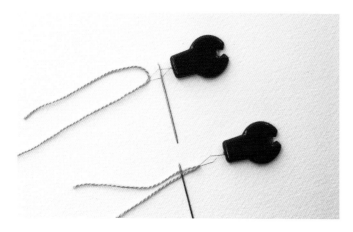

Store-bought needle threader.

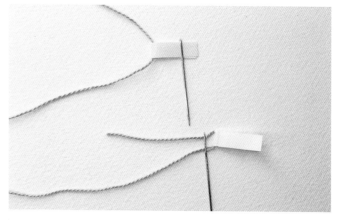

Improvised needle threader.

Stitching Techniques

Embroidery requires very few specific techniques, beyond the way you insert the needle and then bring it out again, and how you secure the thread but, as always, practice makes perfect.

Sewing and stabbing

Stitching involves inserting a needle into the fabric and out again. This may seem straightforward but there are essentially two different methods of doing it – sewing and stabbing – each of which has its own merits. The method you choose is, at the end of the day, down to personal preference. When you are learning a new embroidery stitch, it might be a good idea to try working it using each of the two methods to see what works best for you. The likely outcome is that you will find that some stitches work better for you using the sewing technique – such as running stitch and backstitch – while others work better with stabbing. You may also find that one method works best when the direction of stitching is from right to left while the other works best going from left to right, so you may even find yourself alternating the two methods while working a particular stitch – such as feather stitch or Cretan stitch.

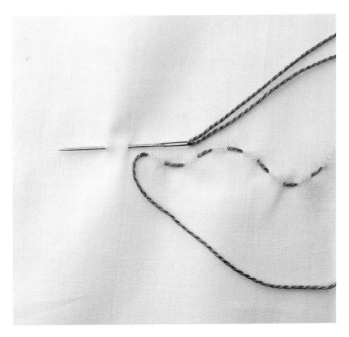

Sewing entails taking the needle in and out of the fabric in a single motion. As the needle scoops up a little of the fabric when using this method, it is usually best done without an embroidery hoop.

Stabbing means taking the needle through the fabric from front to back, then from back to front, in two separate journeys.

Fastening thread to fabric

Some embroiderers start stitching by knotting the end of their thread while others consider this to be bad practice. There are definitely disadvantages in knotting the end of the thread: it can cause a lump, it can show through on the front of the work, it can pull through to the front of the work, and it might actually come undone, causing stitches to unravel.

There are several alternative ways to attach a new thread before starting to stitch, perhaps the most straightforward being the waste knot. This entails knotting the end of the thread and then inserting the needle down through the right side of the fabric, a short distance from the design area, leaving the knot sitting on the surface of the fabric. As you start to stitch, the tail of thread is covered by the stitches on the wrong side, locking the thread in place. Once

the thread has been secured, you can trim off the knot and any excess thread. Of course, once you have stitched an area of the fabric, there should be no need to use the waste knot method: new lengths of thread can be secured under the existing stitches, by passing the needle back and forth under these threads two or more times.

To fasten off a length of thread, when you have finished stitching, take the needle to the wrong side of the work and pass it under the back of the stitches. Make sure it is secure, with no risk of unravelling, then trim off the excess thread. To do this successfully, make sure you stop stitching before the thread becomes too short; you need to have enough left to enable you to take it through to the back and pass it under a sufficient number of stitches.

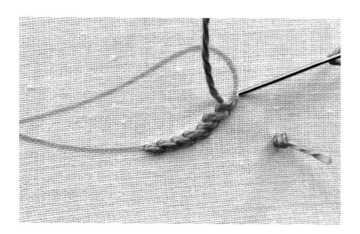

Attaching a new thread using a waste knot.

Fastening off thread on the wrong side of the fabric.

Aftercare

Store finished embroidery pieces flat and in a dark place so that thread colours don't fade. Where practical, lay them unfolded in a box with layers of white acid-free tissue paper. Larger pieces can be rolled around a cardboard tube covered with tissue, right side out, then overwrapped with more tissue. Of course, not all embroidery projects will be stored away and perhaps even forgotten. Hopefully, you will be proud enough of the finished work to wish to frame it or perhaps to make it into a cushion or other item.

Useful Embroidery Terms

appliqué
A technique of attaching fabrics and other materials to a base fabric.

Assisi embroidery
A type of counted-thread embroidery where the outline of a motif is worked in Holbein stitch and the background in cross stitch.

basting
Temporary stitching, also known as tacking, where running stitch is used to join layers of fabric together.

blackwork
Counted-thread embroidery based on backstitch and running stitch worked vertically, horizontally and diagonally, forming geometric patterns, usually worked using black thread.

broderie anglaise
Freestyle embroidery creating a lacy effect of cut holes and small shapes.

canvaswork
Also known as needlepoint, this is a type of counted-thread embroidery, usually worked in woollen threads, and often resembling woven tapestry.

composite stitch
A stitch formed by a combination of two or more basic stitches.

couching
A technique in which threads or other materials are laid across the surface of the fabric ground and held in place with small stitches. Couching threads can match the laid threads or contrast with them.

counted cross stitch
Cross stitch patterns and designs worked on counted-thread fabrics.

crewel work
A type of freestyle embroidery usually worked on linen or woollen fabric using woollen threads or yarns.

cutwork
Embroidery in which parts of the fabric are cut away.

divisible thread
Several strands, usually presented in a loosely twisted skein or wrapped around a card, that can be separated and used singly or re-combined.

embossed work
Another name for embroidery where stitches are raised above the surface of the fabric.

evenweave
A fabric with a distinct plain weave, where each thread is clearly visible. There are the same number of threads per inch (or centimetre) in both directions. Stitches are worked by counting the threads and following the weave of the fabric.

floss
The term for stranded thread, including six-stranded embroidery cotton, generally used in the USA.

freestyle embroidery
Embroidery on plain fabric, created by following design lines rather than counting fabric threads.

ground
This refers to the fabric that provides the background to an embroidery.

Hardanger
Counted-thread embroidery originating in Norway, with groups of satin stitches and drawn threads creating openwork patterns.

hoop
Two rings that fit together, to hold fabric taut.

interlacing
Starting with a foundation of straight stitches, another thread is woven under the stitches to create a laced effect without going through the fabric.

Jacobean
This style of embroidery, typically worked with woollen threads on linen fabric, was popular in the first quarter of the 17th century and usually featured fancy plants and animal motifs.

laid work
This is another term related to couching; it refers to the threads being laid across the surface of the fabric.

monogram
An embroidered motif consisting of letters of the alphabet, usually a person's initials, used to identify or personalise a garment or item of household linen.

mouliné
A French term for stranded embroidery thread, or floss, used by European manufacturers.

perle
A twisted, non-divisible cotton embroidery thread, otherwise referred to as pearl thread or pearl cotton.

plunging
Taking the cut end of a couching thread through the fabric.

ply
Two or more threads twisted together to form a single strand. Plys are not intended to be separated.

shisha
Pieces of mirror glass used mainly in India and Pakistan for embellishing embroideries.

skein
A measured length of thread or yarn loosely twisted together.

smock(ing)
Embroidery stitches worked on fabric that has been gathered into fine pleats. The embroidery stitches hold the pleats securely in place as well as creating decorative patterns and designs.

stabbing
A stitching method that requires two separate hand movements.

stabiliser
A non-woven fabric used to back fabrics while stitching, to create a thicker ground and to prevent any distortion.

surface embroidery
Embroidery in which stitches do not follow the weave of the fabric; sometimes called freestyle embroidery.

synthetic fabric
Fabric made from man-made fibres usually derived from coal and petroleum.

thimble
A finger-cap, usually made from metal, plastic or leather, to protect fingertips from being pricked by sharp needles.

thread count
The number of threads per inch or centimetre; a fine fabric has a high thread count while a coarser fabric has a lower thread count.

tying
The anchoring of a thread to the surface of a fabric, using small stitches.

whitework
Any form of white-on-white embroidery.

working thread
The thread coming out of the fabric, not the cut end that is threaded through the eye of the needle.

Lines and Outlines

Running Stitch

Also known as kantha, sashiko, quilting and tacking stitch, this is the most basic embroidery stitch. Use it for delicate outlining, in single or multiple lines, to join layers of fabric together, for quilting, and as padding under satin stitch, especially where a dark thread is used on a light-coloured fabric (see padded satin stitch, page 104).

◀ *Here sashiko-style running stitch, with the stitches slightly longer than the gaps in between, is used to outline the design, using a non-divisible thread.*

To work running stitch:

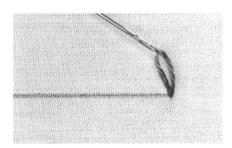

Step 1: Draw a guideline, if you wish. Starting on the right, bring the needle up at the beginning of the line.

Step 2: Working from right to left, make the first stitch by inserting the needle back down into the fabric a stitch length from the beginning and up again a little way along the line.

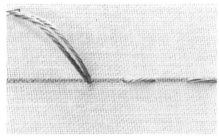

Step 3: Repeat this action all along the stitch line. To make an even line of stitches, the stitches and the gaps in between should be a similar length.

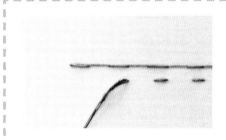

For an open effect, like a dotted or dashed line: Leave longer intervals between stitches.

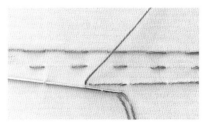

For a more solid line: Pick up just one or two threads of fabric between each stitch.

TIP You can also work from left to right if you find it easier or are left-handed. Try working a few stitches at a time, taking the needle in and out of the fabric at a shallow angle. If you are working with a hoop, use a stabbing motion, taking the needle up through the fabric and pulling it taut before pushing it back down, working one stitch at a time.

Whipped Running Stitch

With a simple embellishment, you can transform a line of plain running stitch into a solid line with a twisted appearance, like a cord. Use the same thread for both operations or, better still, for the whipping use a thread of similar weight but a different colour, or a different type of thread for a textural contrast.

Whipped running stitch outlines this butterfly. The antennae use French knots (page 80) and satin stitch (page 103) is used for the body and head.

To work whipped running stitch:

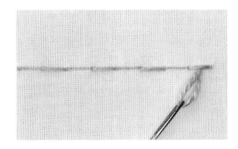

Step 1: Draw a guideline and work a line of running stitch.

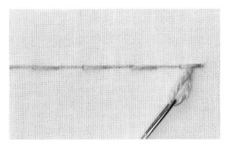

Step 2: Thread your needle with a length of contrasting thread and bring the needle up at the start of the line, below the centre of the first running stitch.

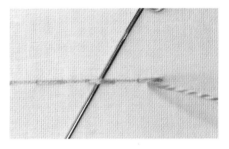

Step 3: Pass the needle under the next stitch, from the top, taking care not to pierce the fabric. Pull the thread through, not too tightly.

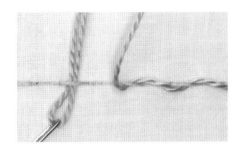

Step 4: Repeat step 3 to the end of the line.

Step 5: To complete the row of stitches, pass the needle down through the fabric above the centre of the last running stitch.

TIP Some stitches involve weaving the needle under previously worked threads without piercing the fabric. To do this, you can try passing the eye of the needle (the blunt end) under the stitch instead of using the sharp needle tip. Alternatively, switch to a blunt-ended tapestry needle (see page 11) to do this part.

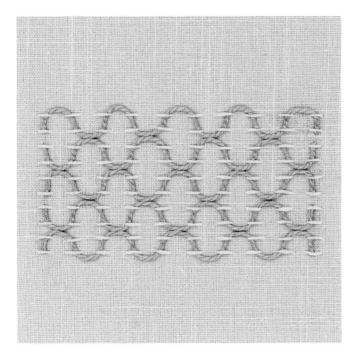

Laced Double Running Stitch

Also known as interlaced running stitch, this is a simple variation of running stitch worked on a foundation of two parallel lines. Useful for when you need a heavier outline, the width can be varied by altering the spacing between the foundation lines. You could also add further lines to make a wider band to make a decorative border or frame.

< *Multiple lines of laced double running stitch make a neat, formal filling or could be worked as a band along a hem.*

To work laced double running stitch:

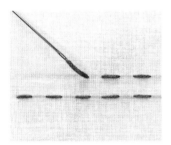

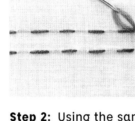

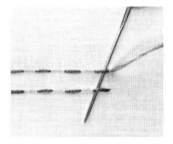

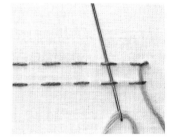

Step 1: Draw two parallel guidelines, if you wish, and work a double row of running stitch (see page 24).

Step 2: Using the same coloured thread, or a contrasting colour or thickness, bring the needle up close to the beginning of the top line.

Step 3: Push the needle downwards under the first thread on both the top and bottom lines, without picking up the fabric, and pull through.

Step 4: Now push the needle up behind the second stitches, once again without picking up the fabric.

Step 5: Working from right to left, repeat step 3 to the end of the line.

Step 6: Take the needle down through the fabric just outside the centre of the last running stitch and fasten off.

TIP To avoid piercing the fabric, use a blunt-tipped needle to work the lacing. You can use the same thread for both the running stitch and the lacing, or choose two contrasting ones. In the steps above, two strands of cotton thread have been used for the running stitches, using a crewel needle. For the lacing stage, all six strands of a contrasting-coloured thread have been threaded into a tapestry needle.

Backstitch

This handy stitch makes a solid line and can be quite fine and delicate or more firm, depending on the thread you use. Backstitch can be used to create straight lines, wavy lines and curves. It is useful for outlining around the edge of a shape and looks good used in combination with most other embroidery stitches.

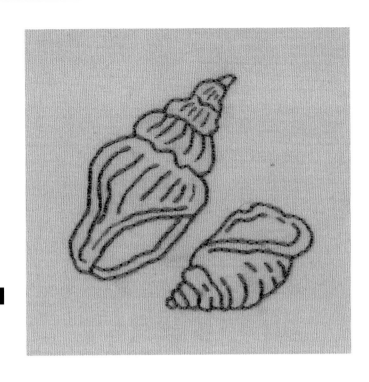

This is the perfect stitch for outlining, as this simple design of seashells shows. Two strands of cotton embroidery thread have been used here, reducing to one strand where a finer line is required.

To work backstitch:

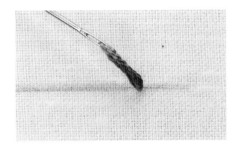

Step 1: Draw a guideline, if you wish, and bring the needle up through the fabric a little to the left of the beginning of the line to be worked.

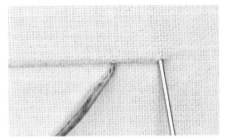

Step 2: Now take the needle back through the fabric at the beginning of the line.

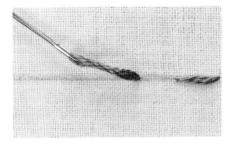

Step 3: Bring the needle up again a stitch length to the left, in front of the place where the needle first emerged.

Step 4: Repeat the process, going back in again at the starting point of each stitch, then forwards, a stitch length in front.

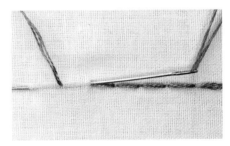

Step 5: You can work backstitch one step at a time, in a stabbing motion, as shown in the previous steps, or you can take the needle tip in and out again in a single step, as shown here.

TIP Backstitch is usually worked from right to left but may be easily worked in the opposite direction if you are left-handed. This may also be true of other stitches, and it is worth experimenting to discover the method that suits you best.

Threaded Backstitch

This creates a slightly wavy line that is most evident when you use two different-coloured threads – one for the line of backstitch and a second for threading through the stitches. The threading technique can also be used on other basic line stitches, such as running stitch (see page 24).

This motif is worked entirely in threaded backstitch, using three strands of cotton thread. For the water, the backstitch is done in blue thread and the lacing in white, to give the impression of little waves.

To work threaded backstitch:

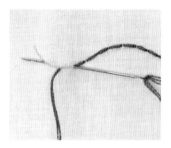

Step 1: Draw a guideline: it can be straight or curved. Bring the needle up through the fabric and work backstitch (see page 27) to the end of the line.

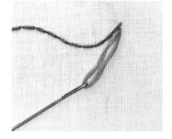

Step 2: Using the same-coloured thread or a contrasting colour, bring the needle up under the first stitch of the backstitch line.

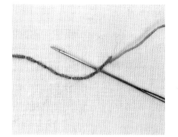

Step 3: Push the needle upwards, under the second stitch. Pull the thread through.

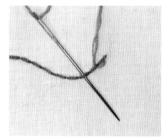

Step 4: Take the needle down through the next stitch, don't pull the thread too tightly. Small loops between stitches look more decorative.

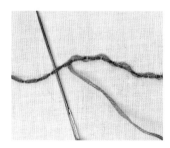

Step 5: Repeat steps 3 and 4 along the line of backstitch.

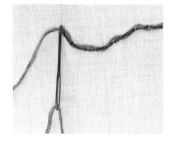

Step 6: Take the needle through the last stitch then back through the fabric. Fasten off on the wrong side.

TIP As with most threading, lacing and whipping, the second thread does not penetrate the fabric but sits on top, held in place by the foundation stitches. If you decide to use a regular embroidery (crewel) needle for this, take care that the sharp point doesn't pick up any of the fabric threads.

Double Threaded Backstitch

This stitch is a simple variation on threaded backstitch and allows you to add a third colour, if you wish. It creates an attractive line that resembles a chain, and it can be worked in a straight line or a gentle curve, making it quite versatile.

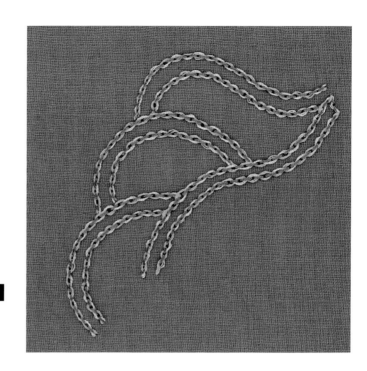

Both the backstitch and the threading are worked using two strands of cotton embroidery thread in a variegated shade. The finished result, chain-like in appearance, provides a neat outline.

To work double threaded backstitch:

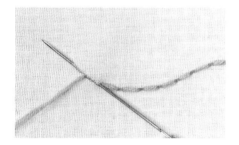

Step 1: Draw a guideline: it can be straight or curved. Bring the needle up through the fabric on the left and work backstitch (see page 27) to the end of the line.

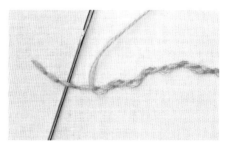

Step 2: Use the same-coloured thread or a contrasting colour to bring the needle up under the first stitch and lace the needle up and down through alternate stitches. See threaded backstitch (page 28).

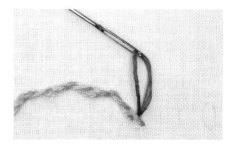

Step 3: Now using a third colour, if you wish, bring the needle up just above the first stitch.

Step 4: Work a second line of lacing, taking the needle under the foundation stitches in the opposite direction to the previous line. Take care not to pull the thread too tightly.

Step 5: At the end of the line, take the needle under the last stitch then down through the fabric close to the centre of this stitch, on the opposite side to the previous thread, and fasten off.

TIP When working the first row of lacing, take care that the needle doesn't pierce the fabric. When working the second row of lacing, make sure not only that the needle doesn't pierce the fabric but also that it doesn't catch on the loops of thread of the previous row of lacing.

Stem Stitch

Also known as stalk, crewel, South Kensington and outline stitch, this popular and useful outline is great for all kinds of applications. It could be used in straight lines, curves, intricate outlines and borders. A line of stem stitch can be made wider by inserting the needle at a more obtuse angle along the guideline. As the name implies, this stitch is useful for embroidering stems. It can also be worked in multiple lines as a filling.

◀ *Simple but effective, these fern-like fronds are embroidered in stem stitch using two strands of cotton thread. You can see how this stitch works well on long and short lines and sinuous curves.*

To work stem stitch:

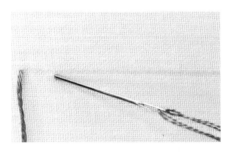

Step 1: Draw a guideline. Working from left to right, bring the needle up at the beginning of the line, then down a stitch length to the right, just below the line.

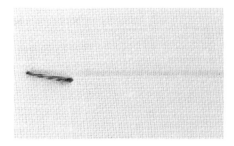

Step 2: Pull the thread through to form the first stitch.

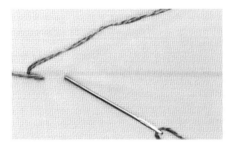

Step 3: Bring the needle up just above the centre of the first stitch, on the guideline, and moving along the line to the right, another stitch length, insert it just below the drawn line.

Step 4: Repeat the process along the whole length of the line, then fasten off.

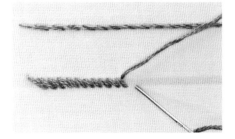

Step 5: You can vary the length of the stitches and increase the slant, to make a thicker line. It may help to draw a thicker guideline in this case.

TIP Here, stem stitch is worked with the thread emerging above the previous stitch. If you change this so that the thread comes out below the previous stitch, the effect is different, with the slope of the stitches reversed, and is known as outline stitch.

Cable Stitch

Similar in appearance to chain stitch, and sometimes called cable chain for this reason, this stitch comprises links joined with short bars. While chain stitch is relatively easy to work, this variation is slightly more tricky because you have to be careful to maintain a good tension on the thread when looping it around the needle in step 5. This stitch can be used for outlining as well as for frames and borders. Evenly spaced, parallel rows of cable stitch make an attractive filling.

Using three strands in a variegated shade, it is easy to see how this stitch differs from chain stitch (page 36) and threaded backstitch (page 28).

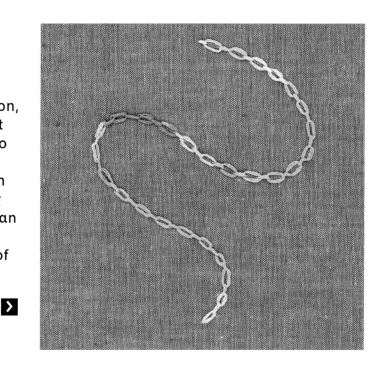

To work cable stitch:

Step 1: Draw a vertical guideline. Working from top to bottom bring the needle up at the top of the line.

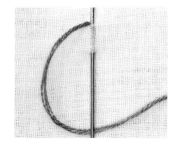

Step 2: Take the needle back down very close the same place and up again a stitch length below. Loop the thread under the tip of the needle.

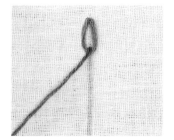

Step 3: Pull the thread through until a small loop – a detached chain stitch – is left on the surface of the fabric.

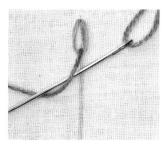

Step 4: Loop the thread once around the tip of the needle.

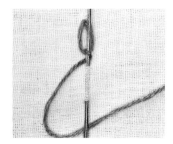

Step 5: Take the needle back down just below the first loop and up again a stitch length below, with the thread under the tip of the needle.

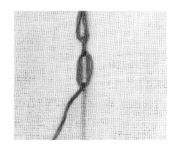

Step 6: Pull the thread, not too tightly, to form a second chain loop or 'link'.

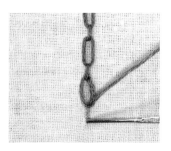

Step 7: Create a series of links with short bars in between. Anchor the last link with a short straight stitch, and fasten off on the wrong side.

TIP For drawing guidelines that will not be covered completely with stitches, you should use an erasable marker (see page 13), otherwise the drawn line will show and spoil the appearance of the finished piece.

Split Stitch

This is a neat and versatile outlining stitch, perfect for straight lines, waves and more intricate shapes and tight curves. It is best worked with the fabric in a hoop and using a stabbing technique (see page 18). Each stitch in turn is split through the centre, producing a fine line with a chain-like appearance. It is also known as Kensington outline stitch.

◀ *Split stitch can be used for intricate outlines, like this bird. You may need to make some of the stitches shorter as they go around a tight curve. The bird's eye is a single French knot (see page 80).*

To work split stitch:

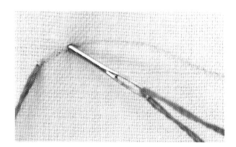

Step 1: Draw a guideline, if you wish. Working from left to right, bring the needle up at the beginning of the line to be worked, then down a stitch length to the right.

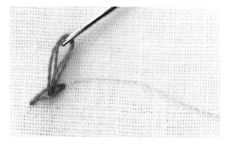

Step 2: Pull the thread through to form the first stitch, then bring the needle up through the centre of the stitch.

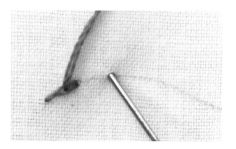

Step 3: Take the needle back down through the fabric, a stitch length to the right.

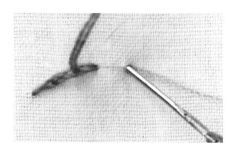

Step 4: Repeat the process for the second and subsequent stitches.

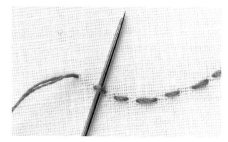

Step 5: When you reach the end of the line, fasten off at the back of the work. You will see that split stitch forms a line of running stitches on the wrong side.

TIP It can be tricky to position the needle on the underside of the fabric. Some people prefer to insert the needle from the top. You can decide which method suits you best. This technique is not, strictly speaking, split stitch but split backstitch, and it uses more thread than the traditional method when you compare the wrong side of the work.

Pekinese Stitch

This is used mostly as an outlining stitch, in single or double rows, depending on the thickness of line you require. It also makes an attractive band or border worked in single or multiple rows. Use thread in two contrasting colours or textures to reveal the intricacy of this stitch, which has a braided appearance. It is related to threaded and double threaded versions of backstitch. It is also known as Chinese stitch, blind stitch and forbidden stitch.

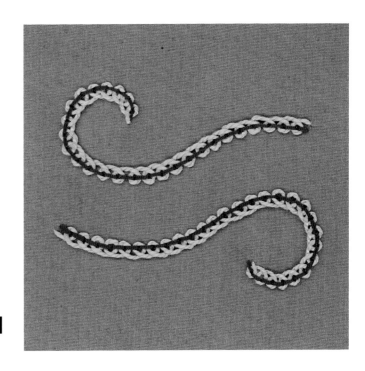

The use of perle thread clearly defines the scrolled effect of the looped stitches.

To work Pekinese stitch:

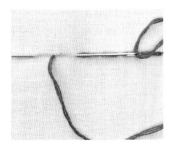

Step 1: Draw a guideline, if you wish. Working from right to left, make a foundation row of backstitch (page 27).

Step 2: With a second thread, bring the needle up through the fabric just below the line of backstitch on the left-hand side.

Step 3: Take the needle upwards under the second stitch of the backstitch line.

Step 4: Push the needle back down through the first stitch. Make sure the tip of the needle passes over the working thread. Pull to tighten.

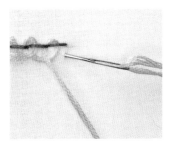

Step 5: Repeat steps 3 and 4 along the line, working from left to right. Pull the thread to tighten the loop after each stitch but not too tightly.

Step 6: At the end of the line, take the needle down through the fabric below the line of backstitch and fasten off on the wrong side.

TIP This is an easy stitch to learn, but the challenge lies in maintaining an even tension. You need to allow small loops to form between the stitches, to emphasise the decorative effect. These loops should be the same size, for a neat finish, so take care when pulling up the thread after each one.

Single Feather Stitch

Related to others in the feather stitch family (but sometimes known as slanted buttonhole stitch), this type produces a broken line that is useful for outlining straight edges and shallow curves; the looped edge can face the inside or outside. You can also work it in multiple rows to create a filling with a delicate lacy effect to combine with other stitches.

❮ *The fern-like effect of single feather stitch can be used for foliage. Here, worked in cotton thread in a variegated shade, it looks like seaweed.*

To work single feather stitch:

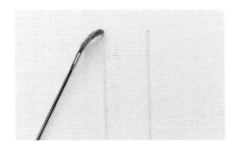

Step 1: Draw a pair of parallel guidelines. Bring the needle out at the top of the left-hand line.

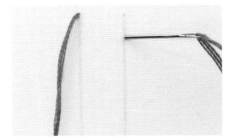

Step 2: Working from top to bottom, take the needle down into the fabric on the right-hand line, a little way down from the top.

Step 3: Bring the needle back up through the fabric on the left-hand line, further down, looping the thread around the needle tip; pull the thread to tighten the loop.

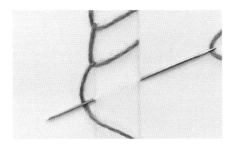

Step 4: Repeat by taking the needle down into the right-hand line, a little way down, then up through the left-hand line in a zigzag fashion, each time catching the loop and pulling the thread.

Step 5: You can alter the width and the distance between stitches. Different threads, such as this perle thread, which has an attractive twist, works well for this type of stitch.

TIP You need to allow small loops to form as you stitch, and it is important to maintain a good tension. If you wish the loops to form on the other side instead, start by bringing your needle up through the right-hand line and down on the left, reversing the effect shown in the steps above.

Cretan Stitch

Cretan stitch is related to feather stitch (see page 46), forming a feathery open zigzag that can be worked in a straight line or a gentle curve, or to fill simple shapes. This stitch comes from the island of Crete, where it is used to decorate garments and household linens. When worked in a straight vertical line, it is sometimes referred to as quill stitch; it is also known as Persian stitch and long-armed feather stitch.

It is easier to work on a fabric with a visible weave, 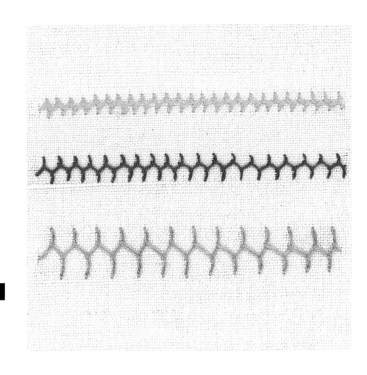 *using it as a guide to produce neat, even lines of stitching. Here, two strands of cotton thread have been used for each row.*

To work Cretan stitch:

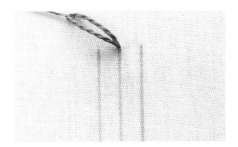

Step 1: Draw three parallel lines, evenly spaced. Bring the needle out at the top of the middle line.

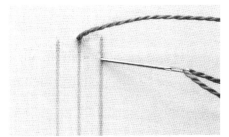

Step 2: Working from top to bottom, take the needle down into the fabric on the right-hand line, a little way below the starting point.

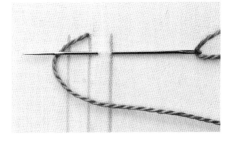

Step 3: Bring the needle back up slightly to the right of the centre line, level with the point on the right-hand line. The thread should be under the tip of the needle. Pull gently to tighten the loop.

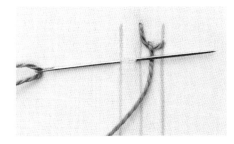

Step 4: Now take the needle into the left-hand line, a little way down, and bring it up slightly to the left of the centre line, level with this point; pull up the thread to create another loop.

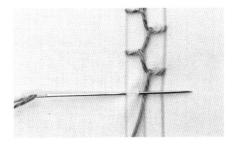

Step 5: Take the needle down alternately into the right-hand line, then into the left-hand line, taking the needle tip over the loop of thread each time.

TIP You need to allow small loops to form as you stitch, and it is important to maintain a good tension. By taking the needle slightly to either side of the centre guideline on alternate stitches, an attractive zigzag stem is formed.

Chain Stitch

In one of the most basic of all embroidery stitches, also known as tambour stitch and point de chainette, cleverly linked loops create a line that resembles a chain. Once you understand the concept of how the stitches are formed and linked, you will find this to be one of the most useful and versatile stitches. It can be used to describe straight or curved lines, and rows of chain stitch can also be worked close together as a filling.

< *The even, lightly textured line formed by chain stitch is perfect for medium-weight outlines such as those in this cactus motif, where the little flower is formed of detached chain (page 74).*

To work chain stitch:

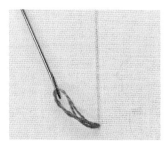

Step 1: Draw a single vertical guideline and bring the needle out at the bottom of the line.

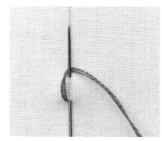

Step 2: Working upwards, push the needle back in at the same point and bring it up a stitch length along with the tip of the needle under the loop.

Step 3: Pull the thread through to form the first stitch.

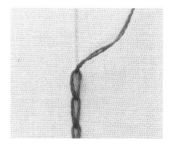

Step 4: Take the needle back down through the loop of the first stitch and out again a stitch length along the line, with the tip of the needle under the loop of thread once again. Repeat this upwards along the length of the line to create a chain of linked loops.

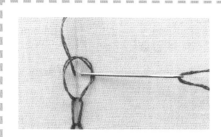

To create a wider chain link: Instead of re-inserting the needle in the same place, bring it out just to the left of the line and insert it just to the right.

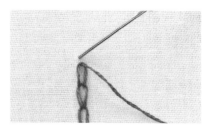

To finish off a line of chain stitch: Secure the last loop of the chain with a short stitch, taking the needle to the back of the work; fasten off.

TIP The stitch is shown here being worked upwards on a vertical line but you can work from top to bottom or from right to left, whichever is easiest for you. Work to an even tension.

Coral Stitch

Effective as a filling when worked in multiple rows, this textured line stitch, resembling a row of fine beads, can be used to form straight or curved lines and outlines and is useful for stems. It is most effective when a rounded thread is used, such as the perle cotton used for the step-by-step instructions below. This stitch is also known as coral knot, knotted stitch, beaded stitch and snail trail.

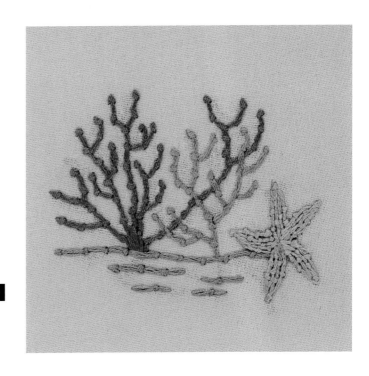

In this undersea motif only coral stitch is used, using three strands of cotton thread. The starfish shape is filled with several lines of coral stitch worked close together and with the knots offset.

To work coral stitch:

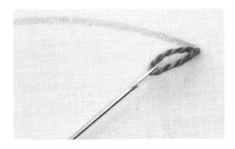

Step 1: Draw a single guideline, which can be a straight line, a wavy line or a shallow curve. Bring the needle out at the beginning of the line, on the right.

Step 2: Working right to left, insert the needle just above the line and bring up just below, picking up a small amount of fabric. The tip of the needle should be over the loop of thread below.

Step 3: Holding the loop of thread to maintain the tension, pull the thread through to form a small knot.

Step 4: Moving the needle along a short way, pick up another small amount of fabric as before, with the working thread looped under the needle tip. Pull through to create another knot.

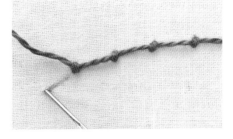

Step 5: Repeat step 4 along the length of the line to create a chain of linked knots. Finish the line with a single straight stitch, taking the needle down into the fabric; fasten off.

TIP This stitch has been given a difficulty rating of three because, as with all knotted stitches, it can be tricky to maintain an even tension and avoid tangling the thread – but it becomes much easier with practice.

Petal Stitch

This attractive stitch combines stem stitch (page 30) with detached chains (page 74). The chain stitches hang down from the line like a row of fairy lights. It can be worked in a straight line, in a curve, in a wavy line or even in a spiral. It is sometimes referred to as petal chain or pendant chain.

◀ *Worked around circular outlines as well as straight lines, using two strands of cotton floss, here the petal stitch looks a little like stalks of barley.*

To work petal stitch:

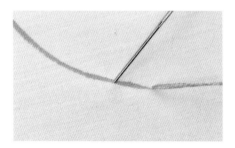

Step 1: Draw a guideline, if you wish. Begin by working a single straight stitch.

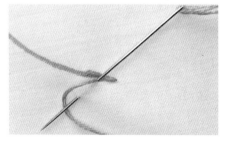

Step 2: Bring the needle up below this stitch, about halfway along, then back in at the same place and out again at a slight slant, with the loop of thread under the tip of the needle.

Step 3: Pull the thread through to form a detached chain, then take the needle into the fabric just below, to form a short stalk and back up a stitch length along the drawn line.

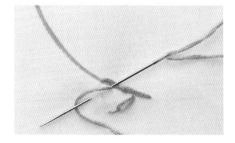

Step 4: Make a backstitch, taking the needle back in below the last stitch and out to the left, halfway along the next stitch and straight below. Make another detached chain at a slant, as before.

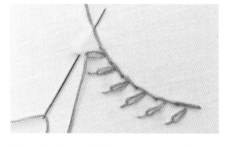

Step 5: Repeat the process along the length of the line.

Rope Stitch

This is a type of knotted stitch that is useful for forming thick outlines. It can be worked in a straight or a curved line. The knots are quite tricky to master but worth persevering with. They are not visible but serve to lift the covering threads to create a raised, textured effect.

This mushroom motif is outlined in rope stitch, using two strands of cotton thread. Finer lines are worked in backstitch using a single strand.

To work rope stitch:

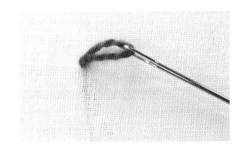

Step 1: Draw a guideline. Bring the needle up through the fabric at the top end of the line.

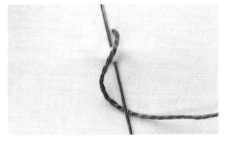

Step 2: Take the needle tip into the fabric a short distance down the line, with the thread on the right, then out again further down the line, forming a loop of thread under the needle tip.

Step 3: Pull the thread through. Now insert the needle just above the chain loop just formed and bring it out again below the chain loop, on the guideline, with the thread looped under the needle tip.

Step 4: Pull through and downwards, to tighten the thread.

Step 5: You will see that a twisted chain loop has been formed, overlapping the previous one.

Step 6: Repeat, working downwards along the line. Finish by taking the thread into the fabric below the last loop and fasten off.

Holbein Stitch

This stitch is a variation of basic running stitch and, if worked in a single colour, resembles backstitch. Unlike backstitch, it is reversible, appearing identical on both the right and wrong sides of the fabric. When worked in two colours, the effect is more decorative. Also known as double running, line and two-sided line stitch, it is used extensively in counted-thread embroidery (notably in blackwork and in Assisi embroidery) but it also works very well as a freestyle stitch.

◀ *Two similar colours have been used for the outline of the mouse and two with a stronger contrast for the horizontal lines.*

To work Holbein stitch:

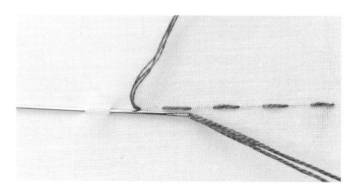

Step 1: Sew a line of running stitch.

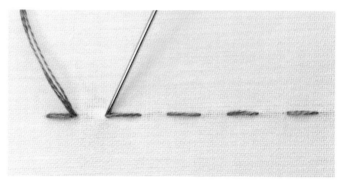

Step 2: Working in the opposite direction, with the same thread, sew a second line of running stitch, which fills the gaps in the first line.

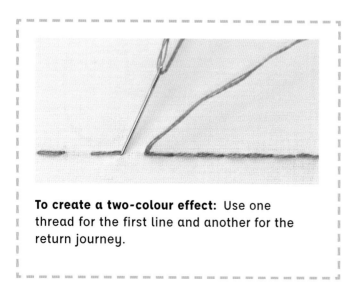

To create a two-colour effect: Use one thread for the first line and another for the return journey.

Blanket Stitch

The difference between blanket stitch and buttonhole is in the spacing of the stitches: blanket stitch, sometimes called open buttonhole, includes gaps between the stitches. It may be familiar as the traditional edging for blankets, which is where it gets its name, and for attaching appliqué shapes, helping to prevent fraying. It is also used as a decorative surface stitch. To vary the effect, try making the uprights different lengths or varying the size of the spaces in between.

Blanket stitch is used as a simple outline here, quick and easy to achieve. The stems and leaf veins are worked in backstitch (see page 27).

To work blanket stitch along a hem:

Step 1: Bring the needle up through the fold at the top edge of the hem. Insert the needle at the base of the hem and bring round the back and up through the loop.

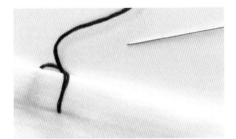

Step 2: Pull up the thread so that the loop sits on the edge of the fold.

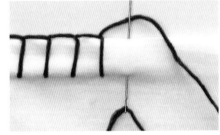

Step 3: Continue in this way, each time ensuring that the thread is in front of the needle so that the loop of thread forms a line across the top fold.

Step 4: To make a line of blanket stitches, repeat the process along the hem.

To work blanket stitch as a decorative surface stitch:
Draw two horizontal parallel lines. Bring the needle up at the start of the upper line. Insert the needle a little way to the right on the lower line, then back up through the upper line immediately above, making sure that the loop of thread is behind the needle; pull through to make the first stitch. Working from left to right, repeat the

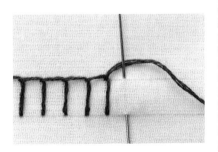

process, taking the needle down on the lower line and up on the top line, creating a small loop each time and spacing the stitches evenly.

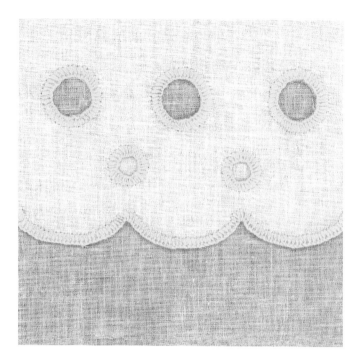

Buttonhole Stitch

Buttonhole stitch is worked along straight lines or curves and has both decorative and practical uses. You can use it for finishing raw edges around holes cut in the fabric, and around the edges of appliqué shapes, to prevent fraying and as a decorative surface stitch. It is the same as blanket stitch but with the stitches placed closer together.

◀ *Close-packed buttonhole stitch allows fabric to be cut close to the stitching without fraying.*

To work buttonhole stitch:

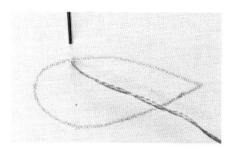

Step 1: Draw a shape. Bring the threaded needle out just below the guideline, then take it down into the fabric above. This distance will determine the width of the outline.

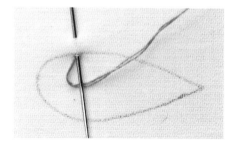

Step 2: Bring the needle back out right next to where it first emerged, with the tip of the needle over the top of the working thread. Pull up the thread to tighten the loop.

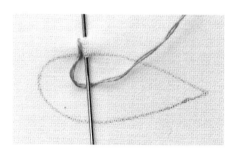

Step 3: For the second and subsequent stitches, take the needle down into the fabric above the line, right next to the previous stitch and back up through the fabric on the lower line next to the previous stitch, so that the stitches lie close together with no gaps in between.

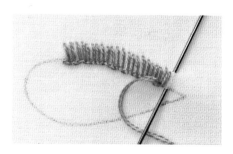

Step 4: Continue in this way until the shape is completely outlined with stitches. Fasten off.

Step 5: If you want to, you can cut away the fabric very close to the stitching.

TIP If you are cutting away the fabric, use small embroidery scissors with sharp pointed blades and take care not to snip the stitches.

Overcast Stitch

This stitch creates a smooth, raised line, like a very fine cord, when worked over a line of backstitch (or other plain outline stitches such as Holbein stitch, close running stitch or split stitch). It is useful for creating bold outlines to shapes.

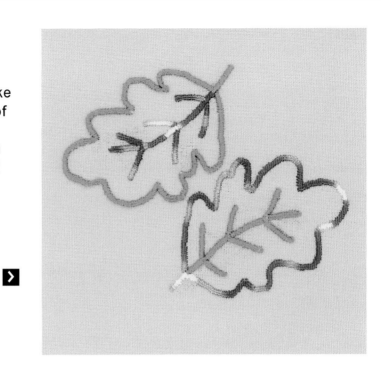

You can see how this stitch forms a neat, raised outline, useful for all kinds of applications. For these leaf shapes, two strands of cotton thread, both plain and variegated, are worked over a backstitch line stitched in perle thread.

To work overcast stitch:

Step 1: Draw guidelines to follow and stretch the fabric in an embroidery hoop. Start by working backstitch along the lines. Perle thread is a good choice for this.

Step 2: Thread a needle with another thread: it's a good idea to use several strands. Bring the needle up close to the foundation stitches, at any point on the outline, just inside the line.

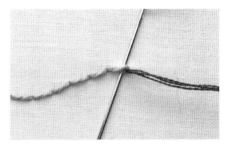

Step 3: Take the needle back down through the fabric on the opposite side of the outline and bring it back out on the inside of the line, close to the previous stitch.

Step 4: Continue like this, working over the foundation outline, to create a neat, cord-like stitch.

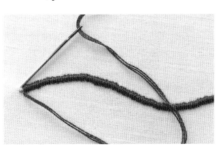

Step 5: Make sure the stitches are worked close together and that the foundation stitches are completely covered.

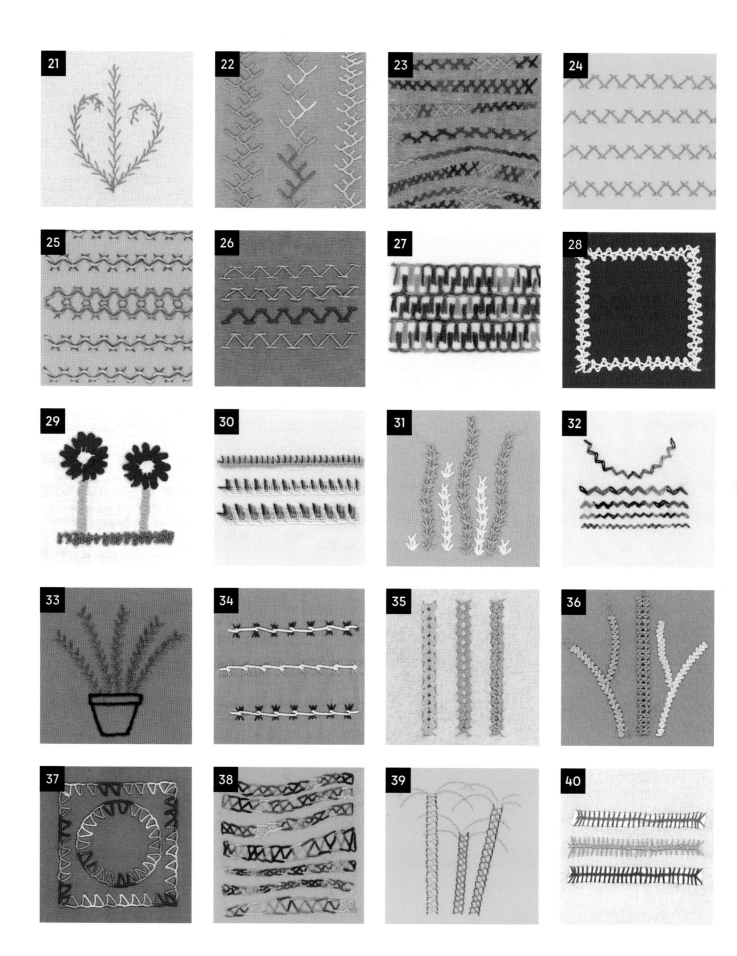

Bands and Borders

Feather Stitch

Historically, feather stitch was used for decorating smocks worn by agricultural workers and it is still one of the most popular and versatile stitches. Use it to create delicate, fern-like fronds in a floral design, as a border, or as a joining or edging stitch in patchwork or quilting. This popular stitch is sometimes known as single coral stitch.

◄ *This fern-like design shows how single rows of feather stitch can be used alone or positioned back to back very effectively.*

To work feather stitch:

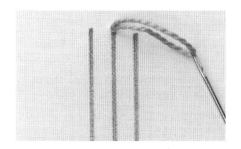

Step 1: Draw three parallel vertical guidelines and bring the needle up at the top of the centre line.

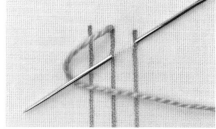

Step 2: Working downwards, push the needle into the right-hand line, a little way down, and bring it back up through the centre line, the same distance further down, looping the thread around the tip.

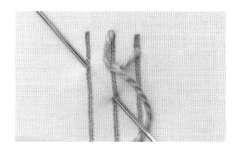

Step 3: Pull the thread to tighten the loop. Take the needle to the left, alongside the last stitch, and bring it back up through the centre line, a little way down, maintaining the same spacing as before. Make sure the thread is beneath the needle tip.

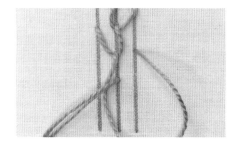

Step 4: Repeat the process, taking the needle down alternately into the right-hand and left-hand lines, bringing it up each time on the centre line.

Step 5: Fasten off by taking the needle over the last loop, creating a small, straight tying stitch.

Double Feather Stitch

One of several variations of feather stitch, and also known as double coral stitch, this is a branched, feathery line that is easy and quick to do. This wider, more ornate line can be worked on straight lines and curves, as a border or worked into a floral design where open, branched patterns are needed. Multiple rows can be used as a lacy filling stitch.

By altering the width of the guidelines and the spacing between stitches, slightly different results can be achieved.

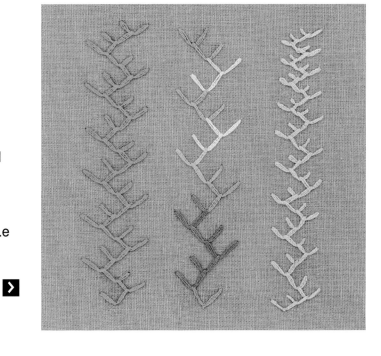

To work double feather stitch:

Step 1: Draw five lines. Bring the needle up at the top of the centre line, push it into the top of the right-hand line and back up on the adjacent line, down a little, looping the thread around the needle tip.

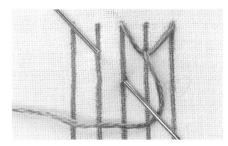

Step 2: Pull through and take the needle down the next line to the left, slightly downwards. Bring it back up through the centre line as before. The thread is beneath the needle tip to create another loop.

Step 3: For the next stitch, take the needle down to the left, in the same way. These three stitches should form a slope. You have now created three loops descending towards the left.

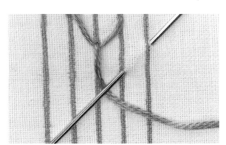

Step 4: Make two more stitches in the same way, this time working towards the right.

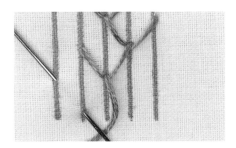

Step 5: Continue in this way, zigzagging from one side to the other, making two stitches each time, working downwards and maintaining equal spaces between the stitches.

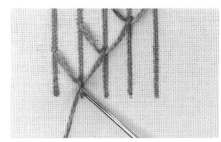

Step 6: Fasten off by taking the needle over the last loop, creating a small, straight tying stitch.

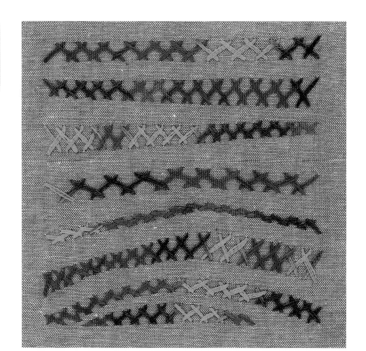

Herringbone Stitch

This popular border stitch forms a crossed zigzag line that can be worked on plain or even-weave fabrics. When using an even-weave, count the threads; when using a plain fabric, draw two parallel lines as a guide. Other names for this stitch include plaited stitch, catch stitch, fishnet stitch, witch stitch, Persian stitch and Russian cross stitch.

◀ *These lines of herringbone stitch are worked using three strands of cotton thread in a variegated shade to achieve different effects.*

To work herringbone stitch:

Step 1: Draw two parallel horizontal guidelines. Bring the needle up through the fabric on the lower line.

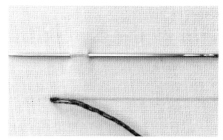

Step 2: Take the needle diagonally up to the upper line and insert it from right to left, bringing it out halfway between the point at which you inserted it and the end of the line.

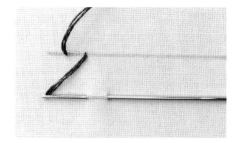

Step 3: You will now have a short horizontal stitch on the wrong side of the fabric. Make a second horizontal stitch in a similar way, this time on the lower line.

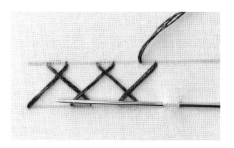

Step 4: Continue in this way, spacing subsequent stitches evenly. The stitches will form a criss-cross pattern on the right side as you move along the line.

TIP This is a useful stitch for fancy couching (see page 113), where it can be worked over a length of thread or ribbon to hold it in place.

Tied Herringbone

A simple variation of herringbone stitch, this offers the opportunity to introduce a second colour for a more fancy effect. It can be used as a lovely neat border that is easy and quick to do, with some scope for combining thread textures and colours. It is also known as coral knotted herringbone stitch.

Both the herringbone stitches and the small tying stitches have been worked using two strands of cotton embroidery thread, with contrasting colours highlighting the stitch to good advantage.

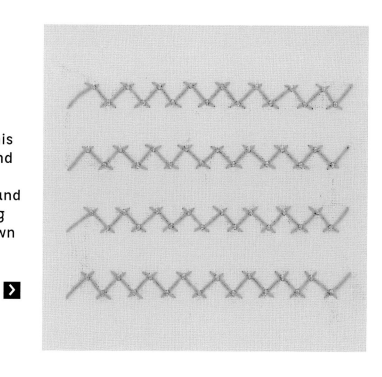

To work tied herringbone:

Step 1: Draw two parallel horizontal guidelines and work a line of herringbone stitch (see page 48), working from left to right.

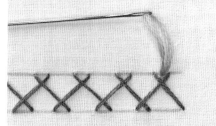

Step 2: Using the same or a contrasting thread, come up through the fabric just above the first intersection of crossed threads at the right-hand end of the line.

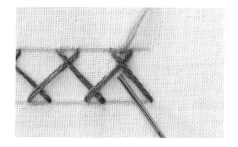

Step 3: Take the needle back down through the fabric below the intersection, forming a short stitch that holds the two crossed threads in place.

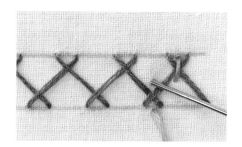

Step 4: Bring the needle up just below the next intersection and take it back down just above.

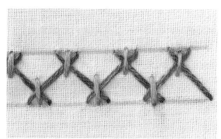

Step 5: Repeat the process, coming up above the crossed threads on the upper line and below the crossed threads on the lower line.

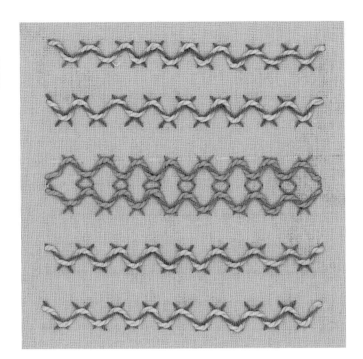

Interlaced Herringbone

Otherwise known as Armenian cross stitch, this lightly textured stitch can be used for neat borders on a hem or as a frame, especially when combined with other decorative bands. Alternatively, it can be used in multiple rows, closely spaced, as an ornate filling.

> ❮ *Here, two strands of cotton embroidery thread have been used for the herringbone foundation stitches and perle thread for the lacing, providing a contrast of texture and colour.*

To work interlaced herringbone:

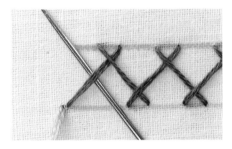

Step 1: Draw two parallel horizontal guidelines using an erasable marker. Work a line of herringbone stitch (see page 48) between the lines.

Step 2: With the same or a contrasting thread and a blunt needle, bring the needle up at the base of the first stitch on the left-hand side.

Step 3: Push the needle upwards under this first stitch, from right to left, without piercing the fabric.

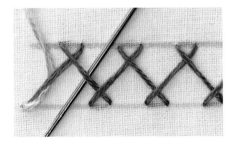

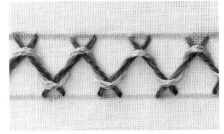

Step 4: Push the needle downwards under the next stitch, from right to left.

Step 5: Repeat the process along the row, then take the needle down through the fabric and fasten off on the wrong side.

TIP Using a blunt needle for the lacing helps to avoid splitting the threads of the foundation stitches or piercing the fabric.

Chevron Stitch

Used on both plain and even-weave fabrics (and in smocking, across the tiny pleats) chevron stitch forms a zigzag line similar in appearance to herringbone (see page 48). It is best worked in a straight line or a very shallow curve. It is a quick and easy stitch for a narrow border; for a wider border, stitch multiple rows or use it in combination with other stitches.

Being such a simple stitch, there is little scope for variation, although different threads create different effects. Shown here from top to bottom: coton à broder, perle, three strands of satin thread and three strands of cotton embroidery thread.

To work chevron stitch:

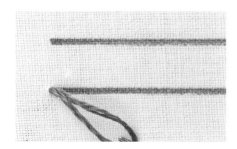

Step 1: Draw two parallel horizontal guidelines. Bring the needle up at the beginning of the lower line.

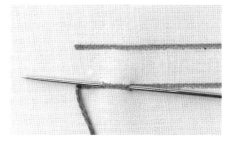

Step 2: Take the needle down through the fabric a stitch length to the right, then bring it up just above the centre of the first stitch, on the guideline. Pull through.

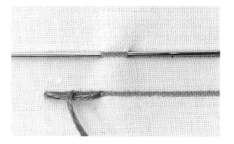

Step 3: Insert the needle on the upper line, from right to left, a little way along to the right, and bring it out a half-stitch length along to the left. This will form a right-sloping diagonal stitch.

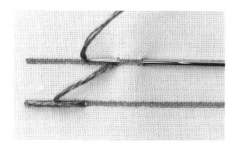

Step 4: Insert the needle at the top of the diagonal stitch and bring it out a half-stitch length to the right.

Step 5: Repeat the process, working from left to right and alternating between the lower and upper lines.

TIP Each time you form a stitch, make sure that the working thread is in the right position. When working horizontal stitches on the lower line, the thread should be below this line; when working horizontal stitches on the upper line, the thread should be above this line.

Double Buttonhole Stitch

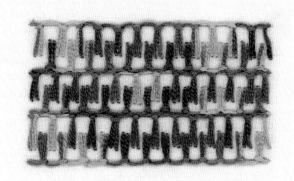

Double buttonhole stitch is a variation of buttonhole or blanket stitch (see page 41, 42); it's also known as double blanket stitch, up-and-down buttonhole or blanket stitch. Each stitch is worked in two stages, forming a double upright. It takes a bit of practice to get right but makes an attractive band or border and can also be used along a hem.

◀ *On repeated rows of double buttonhole stitch, a variegated thread adds visual interest and helps to draw attention to the unusual structure.*

To work double buttonhole stitch:

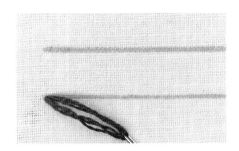

Step 1: Draw two parallel guidelines. Bring the needle up at the left, on the lower line.

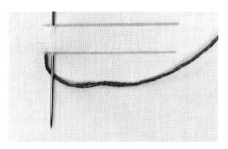

Step 2: Take the needle down through the fabric on the upper line, a little to the right, and bring it back up through the lower line, just below. Make sure the thread is looped under the needle tip.

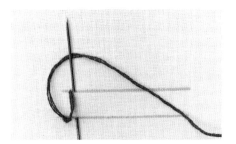

Step 3: Insert the needle into the lower line, next to the last stitch, and up through the upper line, with the thread looped underneath. Pull it downwards: a small horizontal stitch will form on the lower line.

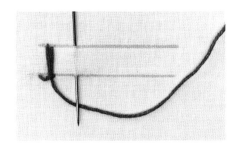

Step 4: Insert the needle into the upper line, a little distance to the right, and bring it out through the lower line, immediately below, with the thread looped under the needle tip.

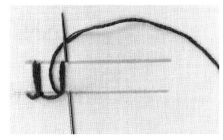

Step 5: Insert the needle into the lower line, next to the previous stitch, and bring it out on the upper line, with the thread looped under the needle tip. Pull through, pulling the needle downwards.

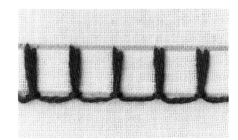

Step 6: Repeat steps 4 and 5 along the row. When you get to the end, take the needle down through the fabric a little way to the right of the lower line.

Spanish Knotted Feather

This very ornamental stitch, also known as twisted zigzag chain, is tricky to get right but it is worth the effort, as it forms a unique braided effect, ideal for decorative borders and outlining.

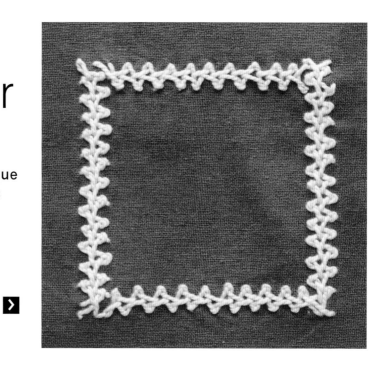

Worked in perle thread, here Spanish knotted feather stitch has been used to create a square frame.

To work Spanish knotted feather:

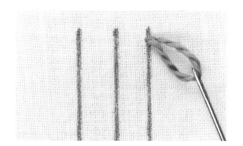

Step 1: Draw three parallel vertical lines using an erasable marker. This stitch is worked from the top downwards. Bring the needle up just below the top of the right-hand line.

Step 2: Insert the needle into the top of the centre line and bring it down diagonally, emerging a little way down the left-hand line. Take the thread over the needle and back under the tip.

Step 3: Pull the thread through; you will see that a twisted chain stitch has been formed.

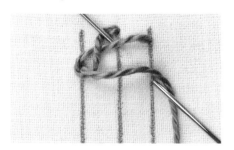

Step 4: Take the needle into the fabric on the centre line, inside the point where the threads cross, and bring it out on the right-hand line. Wrap the thread around the needle to form a twisted chain stitch.

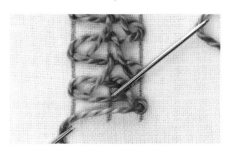

Step 5: Repeat the process, alternating from right to left, each time forming a diagonal stitch.

TIP Each time you make a stitch, ensure that the needle enters the fabric at the intersection of the previous stitch, just next to where the threads that form the twisted chain cross over each other.

Rosette Chain

Forming a decorative braided line, this fancy border stitch, as with any stitch that incorporates a knot or twist, is tricky to get right and requires a bit of practice to achieve a neat effect. Work it along a straight line, such as a hemline, or a shallow curve. It can also be worked in a circle to create a floral motif. Other names for this stitch include bead edging stitch and wrapped coral stitch.

You can see from this example that this stitch is useful for straight lines, creating a braided band, and can also be worked in a circle to make an attractive flower head.

To work rosette chain:

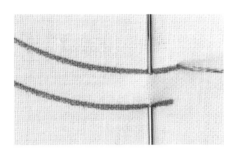

Step 1: Draw two horizontal lines, straight or curved. Bring the needle out on the right-hand end of the upper line, take it into the same line to the left, then back out on the lower line immediately below.

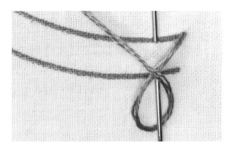

Step 2: Loop the thread around the tip of the needle from left to right.

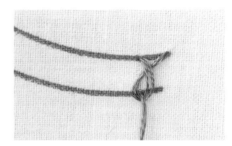

Step 3: Pull the thread through, not too tightly; you will see that a twisted chain stitch has now been formed.

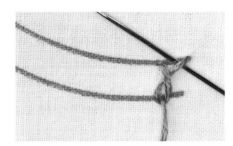

Step 4: Take the needle under the right-hand thread of the twisted chain without piercing the fabric; pull through.

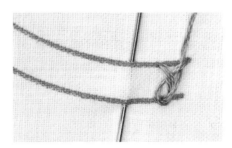

Step 5: Insert the needle into the upper line a short distance to the left and bring it out again on bottom line, immediately below, as you did in step 1.

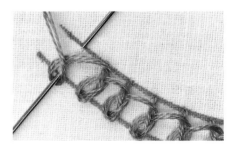

Step 6: Now repeat the process of forming a twisted chain, taking the needle under the thread and moving left along the guidelines, stitch by stitch.

Overlapping Blanket Stitch

Also known as encroaching blanket stitch, this variation offers the opportunity to use multiple colours and to create bands of stitching of different widths. It makes a pleasing border and is usually worked in a straight line.

Using two strands of cotton embroidery thread, you can see the different results that can be achieved using (from top to bottom) three, five and seven overlapping lines of blanket stitch in a range of colours, creating a kind of 3D effect.

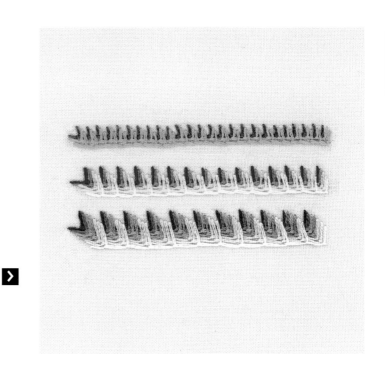

To work overlapping blanket stitch:

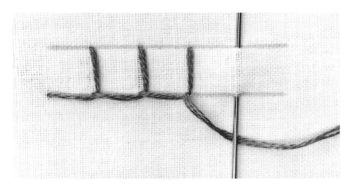

Step 1: Work a line of blanket stitch (see page 41), with the stitches evenly spaced.

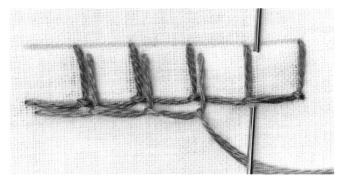

Step 2: With the same thread or a contrasting colour, work a second line of blanket stitch, just below the first and overlapping it, placing the uprights directly to the right of those on the first row.

Step 3: If you wish, you can work additional rows, each offset from the last, placing the upright part of each stitch to the right of those in the previous row each time.

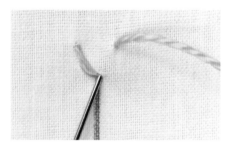

Wheatear Stitch

A variation of chain stitch (see page 36), this produces an effect like stalks of wheat or corn – hence the name. Worked as a detached or isolated stitch, it can be used for seeding, which involves scattering individual stitches over an area, or as an open filling. A single stitch is intended to represent an ear of wheat and is a good companion to other small isolated stitches such as tête de boeuf (see page 76).

> Easy to work, this stitch produces quick results. It is particularly effective when worked in a smooth thread such as perle, as it is here.

To work wheatear stitch:

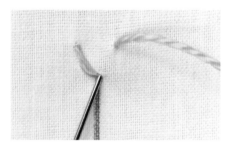

Step 1: Draw a guideline. Bring the needle up just above and to the left, insert it into the top of the line, come up again above and to the right, then down again into the top of the line, forming a 'V'.

Step 2: Bring the needle up again, a little way down the line, then pass it from right to left under the ends of the first two stitches without picking up any fabric.

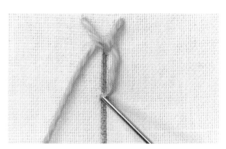

Step 3: Repeat this action all along the stitch line. To make an even line of stitches, the stitches and the gaps in between should be a similar length.

Step 4: Work two straight stitches, in a 'V' formation, into the base of the chain loop, then make another chain, taking the needle under the strands of the previous stitch.

Step 5: To make a line of stitches, repeat the process along the drawn line, working downwards.

TIP You can make both the V-shaped stitch and the chain longer or wider, to vary the appearance of the stitch – but make sure the stitches and the gaps in between remain consistent.

Zigzag Chain

A simple variation of chain stitch, also known as Vandyke chain, this makes a neat border or outline and can also be used, in multiple lines, as an open filling. Any type of embroidery thread can be used for this stitch.

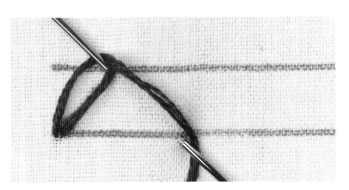

For different widths of zigzag chain, different numbers of stranded thread have been used here, with just a single strand for the narrowest band.

To work zigzag chain:

Step 1: Draw two parallel guidelines. Bring the threaded needle out on one of the lines and make a single chain stitch (see page 36) across the two lines and at an angle of 45 degrees.

Step 2: Insert the needle back down into the same place, in the loop of the previous stitch, and bring it out again on the opposite guideline, making another stitch at a 45-degree angle.

....

TIP When drawing guidelines for this or any stitch that will not completely cover the lines, be sure to use a marker that can be erased or that will naturally fade away.

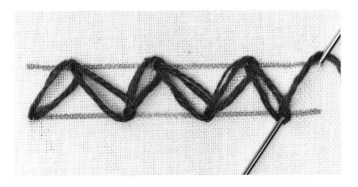

Step 3: Carry on like this, repeating step 2 and working from right to left along the guidelines. The chain stitches will form a zigzag with each stitch at right angles to the next.

Feathered Chain

This simple variation of basic chain stitch (see page 36), sometimes called chained feather stitch, creates an attractive zigzag line. Worked between two parallel lines, it could be placed along a hemline or the edge of a collar, used to make a frame or to create wide stems in a bold floral design.

Using three strands of cotton embroidery thread, gently curved lines of feathered chain form fern-like branches. The pot is outlined in split stitch.

To work feathered chain:

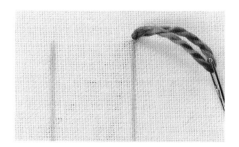

Step 1: Draw two parallel guidelines with an erasable marker. Bring the needle out at the top of the right-hand line.

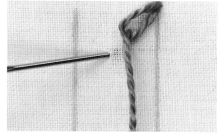

Step 2: Start by stitching a detached chain with a long tail ending slightly to the left of the mid-point between the lines; angle it at about 45 degrees.

Step 3: Bring the needle out on the left-hand line and work another chain, with its base at the end of the previous stitch's tail and the tail ending between the left-hand line and a point to the left of centre.

TIP If you find it helpful when positioning the stitch tails, you could draw a third guideline down the centre.

Step 4: Repeat this process, with the stitches connected as shown, to form a zigzag.

Step 5: When you reach the bottom of the line, take the needle through to the wrong side, at the end of the tail, and fasten off.

Butterfly Chain

This stitch is formed in two stages and can be worked in a single colour or with two contrasting threads. It forms a pretty, feathery line that can be used singly for a simple border or outline or combined with other stitches.

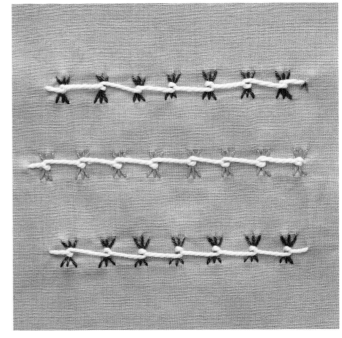

The foundation stitches have been worked using two strands of cotton embroidery thread and the tying stitches using perle thread.

To work butterfly chain:

Step 1: Draw two horizontal parallel guidelines. Between these lines, work a series of three grouped vertical straight stitches, evenly spaced.

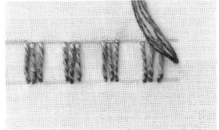

Step 2: Thread a blunt needle with the same or a contrasting thread. Bring the needle up through the fabric to the right of the line of foundation stitches, halfway between the drawn lines.

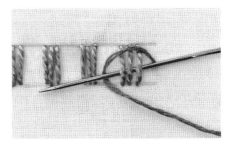

Step 3: Take the thread across the first group of three stitches, then take it under the stitches and through the loop formed by the thread.

Step 4: Pull up the thread to tighten the knot around the three stitches, pulling them into a bundle.

Step 5: Repeat the process, working from right to left across the row. Finish by inserting the needle to the left of the last bundle and fasten off on the wrong side.

TIP This is one of those stitches where left-handers may prefer to work the row by starting at the left of the line, rather than the right.

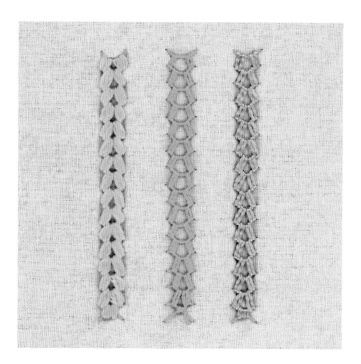

Portuguese Border Stitch

This woven stitch creates a raised, braid-like band that sits on the surface of the fabric. Ladder-like horizontal stitches form the foundation and a second thread is wrapped around these 'rungs' without piercing the fabric. Any thread can be used, depending on the effect you wish to create.

◄ *These foundation stitches have all been made using two strands of cotton thread. The lacing uses other threads, showing how different effects can be achieved.*

To work Portuguese border stitch:

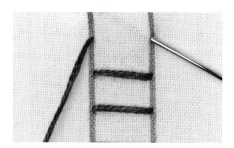

Step 1: Using an erasable marker, draw two vertical parallel lines and work evenly spaced parallel horizontal stitches from bottom to top, like rungs of a ladder.

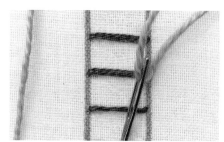

Step 2: Bring the needle up through the fabric below the first horizontal stitch. Take the needle down behind the second and first stitches without piercing the fabric; repeat twice more.

Step 3: Now take the needle down behind the second foundation stitch only, again without piercing the fabric, coming out on the left-hand side.

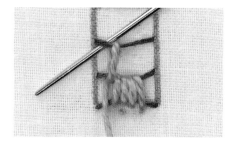

Step 4: Pass the needle under the third and second foundation stitches once, then under the third stitch only.

Step 5: Following the process in step 4, pass the needle under the fourth and third stitches, then the fourth only; under the fifth and fourth, then the fifth only, and so on, up to the top. Fasten off.

Step 6: To complete the other side, bring the needle up below the second foundation stitch, on the right, and repeat the process with stitches slanting the other way.

Raised Chain Band

This stitch forms an attractive, raised braid-like band. It can be worked using any thread, but a firm, twisted thread such as perle is a good choice as it produces an even texture that is particularly effective. It can be worked in a single shade or in two contrasting colours. Use it for straight lines or gentle curves.

This textured stitch can be worked in a straight or curved line. In the centre, two adjacent lines of stitching create a wider band.

To work a raised chain band:

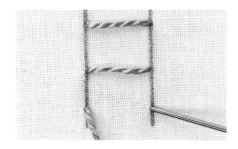

Step 1: Draw two parallel vertical guidelines and work a foundation of evenly spaced horizontal stitches between them.

Step 2: Bring the needle up through the fabric above the middle of the top stitch. Pass the needle over the stitch, then under it from below, with the needle pointing to the left. Pull through.

Step 3: Loop the thread under the stitch, then take the needle under the foundation stitch from above, to the right of the first raised chain, and over the loop of thread, with the needle pointing to the left.

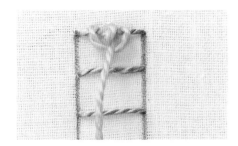

Step 4: Pull the thread through to tighten the stitch.

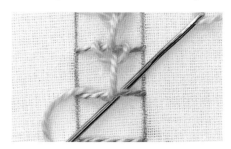

Step 5: Repeat the process for each foundation stitch, working from top to bottom.

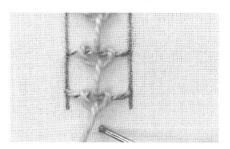

Step 6: Finish by taking the needle through the fabric below the last foundation stitch and fasten off.

Closed Blanket Stitch

An attractive stitch for decorating hems and creating borders and frames, this blanket stitch variation, also known as closed buttonhole stitch, is easy to do. Blanket stitches are worked in pairs, forming a row of neat triangles.

Using a variegated perle thread, closed blanket stitch is worked as an outline around geometric shapes to form neat frames.

To work closed blanket stitch:

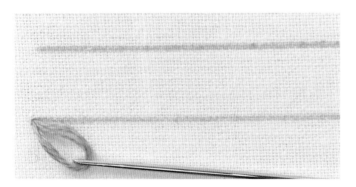

Step 1: Draw two parallel guidelines. Bring the needle up on the left-hand side of the lower line.

Step 2: Work a blanket stitch at a slant, taking the needle down into the fabric a little way along the upper line and bringing it up just to the right of where it first emerged, with the thread under the needle.

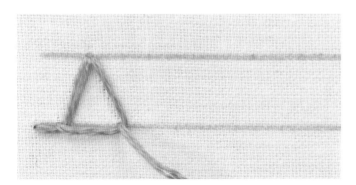

Step 3: Work a second stitch, taking the needle down into the same place on the upper line and bringing it back up on the lower line to form a diagonal sloping in the other direction.

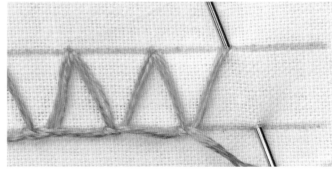

Step 4: Continue working pairs of stitches along the line, with each pair forming a triangle.

Closed Feather Stitch

For lines of varying widths, straight or curved, this is a straightforward stitch, a variation of feather stitch where each stitch touches the previous one, creating a pattern of joined triangles.

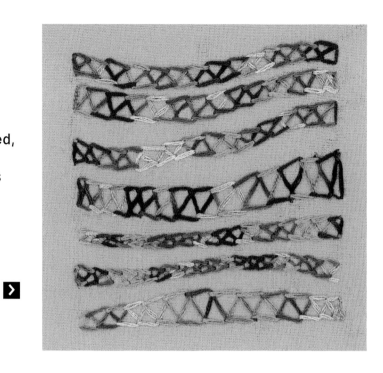

Varying the width and spacing of lines of closed feather stitch creates subtle variations. Here three strands of a variegated cotton thread have been used.

To work closed feather stitch:

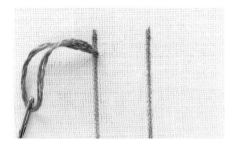

Step 1: Draw two parallel vertical guidelines. Bring the needle up through the fabric towards the top of the left-hand line.

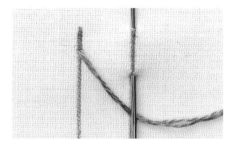

Step 2: Take the needle down through the top of the right-hand line and bring it back up a little way below. Make sure the thread is under the tip of the needle. Pull through.

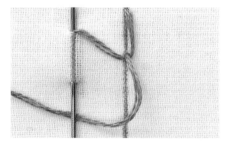

Step 3: Loop the thread, then take the needle in again on the left-hand line where the thread first emerged and bring it out a stitch length below, with the needle tip inside the loop. Pull through.

Step 4: Continue in this way, working downwards and creating stitches first on one side and then on the other.

Step 5: At the base, secure the last loop with a small stitch and fasten off on the wrong side.

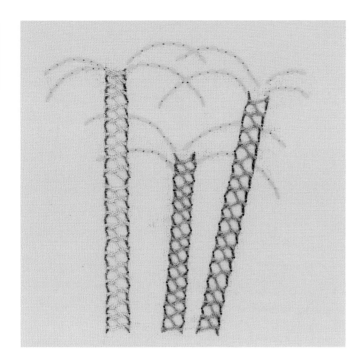

Herringbone Ladder Stitch

This decorative lattice band can be worked in a single colour or two contrasting shades to create simple bands and borders, alone or in combination with other stitches.

◀ *Using two strands of cotton embroidery thread, the stitch has been used to describe tree trunks, with curved lines of foliage added in backstitch.*

To work herringbone ladder stitch:

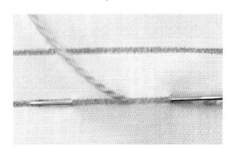

Step 1: Draw two parallel guidelines. Work backstitch (see page 27) along one of the lines.

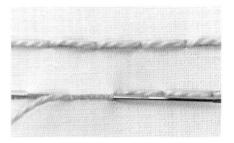

Step 2: Now work backstitch along the second line, offsetting the stitches so that the ends of the stitches on the second line correspond to the stitch centres on the first line.

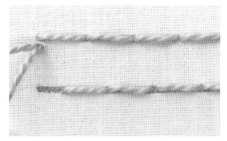

Step 3: Thread a blunt needle with the same or a contrasting thread. Bring the needle up through the fabric at the top left, just below the first backstitch.

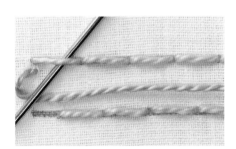

Step 4: Pass the needle downwards, under the first backstitch, with the needle tip over the loop of thread. Pull through.

Step 5: Now pass the needle up under the first backstitch on the lower line, crossing over the thread.

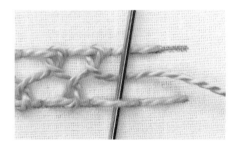

Step 6: Repeat, taking the needle down through each stitch in turn on the upper line and bringing it up through each stitch on the lower line, crossing over the thread each time.

Vandyke Stitch

This woven stitch creates a decorative band when worked in a straight line – but it can also be worked across a simple shape such as a leaf or petal. Because of the way that stitches are laced down the centre without piercing the fabric, it also makes an effective couching stitch worked over lengths of ribbon.

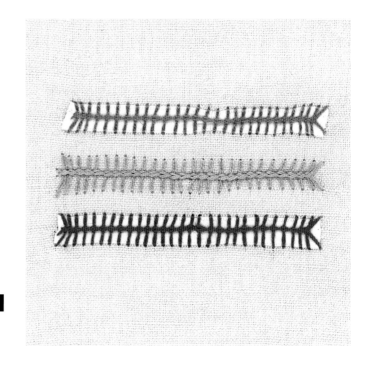

The central row is worked straight onto the fabric, while the top and bottom rows have been worked over lengths of ribbon, like a fancy couching stitch.

To work Vandyke stitch:

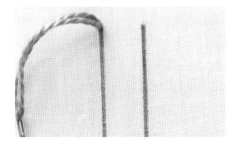

Step 1: Draw two parallel lines, using an erasable marker. Bring the needle out through the fabric at the top of the left-hand line.

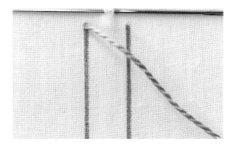

Step 2: Make a small stitch from right to left, above the centre of the design area, to form an anchor for subsequent stitches.

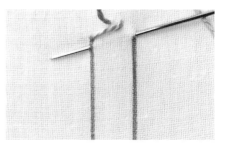

Step 3: Insert the needle into the top of the right-hand line and bring it back out on the left, just below the previous stitch.

Step 4: Take the needle under the loops of the centre stitch.

Step 5: Now insert the needle back on the right-hand line and bring it out on the left, maintaining the same spacing as before.

Step 6: Repeat the two-stage process, working downwards and taking the needle under the central thread loops each time, creating a kind of plaited braid down the centre.

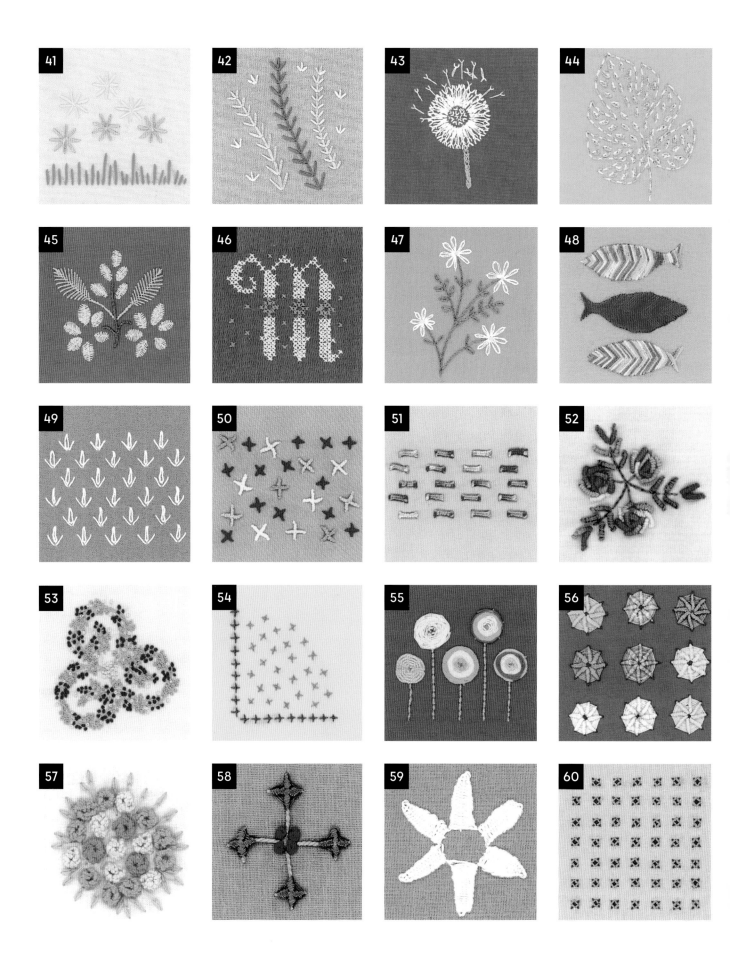

Isolated Stitches and Motifs

Straight Stitch

So simple, it hardly merits a separate entry, this stitch should not be overlooked or underestimated as it forms the foundation of so many other stitches, such as running stitch (page 24), fern stitch (page 69) and countless more. Use it to create areas of texture or to depict leaves, grasses and other small details. It is sometimes called single satin stitch.

◄ *Perfect for blades of grass and dainty petals, as well as more abstract applications, straight stitch could not be easier to work.*

To work a straight stitch:

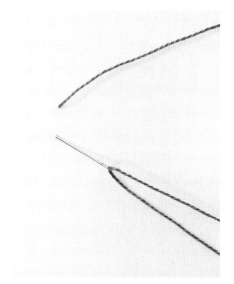  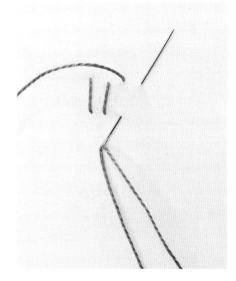

Step 1: Bring the needle up through the fabric and back down a stitch length away.

Step 2: Pull the thread through to create a single straight stitch.

Step 3: When working a number of straight stitches, work each one in the same direction as the last.

Fern Stitch

Extremely easy to work, fern stitch can be used as an isolated stitch or repeated along a guideline to make an attractive branched stem. It is useful for outlining or for representing sprays of foliage or leaf veins.

Make lines of fern stitches all the same size, or progressively longer as you work down the stem.

To work a single fern stitch:

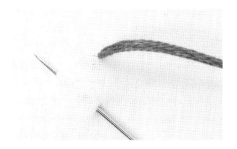

Step 1: First make a vertical straight stitch, bringing the needle out again to the left, the same distance away as the first stitch.

Step 2: Take the needle down into the base of the first stitch and out again the same stitch length to the right.

Step 3: Take the needle back down into the same place as before, to complete the stitch.

To work a line of fern stitches:

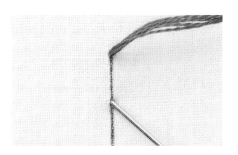

Step 1: Draw a single guideline, which will form the stem. Bring the needle up at the top of the line and insert it a stitch length below, on the line.

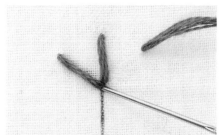

Step 2: Bring it out to the left, and down into the base of the vertical stitch, then out to the right and back into the base of the vertical stitch.

Step 3: Continue making linked fern stitches in this way, working from top to bottom on the guideline.

Fly Stitch

This basic stitch, also known as Y stitch and open loop stitch, can be worked singly or in groups, overlapped or evenly scattered as a light filling. It can also be worked in rows: a vertical line, with each stitch touching the next, can resemble a feather or the veins of a leaf. Alter the look by increasing the length of the anchoring stitch.

◀ *For this dandelion clock, fly stitch has been used throughout: even the stalk is formed of a vertical line of fly stitches worked close together.*

To work fly stitch:

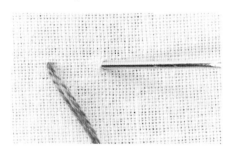

Step 1: Bring the needle through at the top left of the position where you want the stitch and insert it back into the fabric a little distance to the right.

Step 2: Pull the thread through but do not pull it tight: leave a little loop.

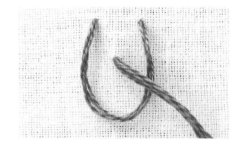

Step 3: Bring the needle back up through the fabric below the other two points and halfway between them. The needle tip should come up through the loop and should point downwards.

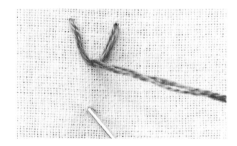

Step 4: Pull the needle through over the thread, forming a V-shape. Work a straight stitch to anchor the loop in place: do this by pushing the needle down into the fabric below the base of the 'V'.

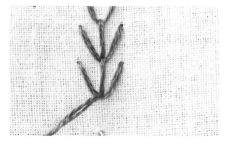

Step 5: Make subsequent stitches following steps 1 to 4. You can isolate each stitch or work stitches close together, to form rows.

TIP Fly stitch can be worked in any direction; it doesn't need to sit upright, like a letter 'Y'.

Swedish Split Stitch

This two-coloured stitch, also known as detached split stitch, can be used as an isolated stitch or accent. It can also be arranged in a group, radiating out from a central point to form a little flower. It is useful as an open filling – or seeding – where you scatter individual stitches over an area or within an outline.

Using perle thread in two colours, the outline of this ▶ *leaf motif is worked in Holbein stitch (see page 40) and Swedish split stitch is used as a scattered filling.*

To work a Swedish split stitch:

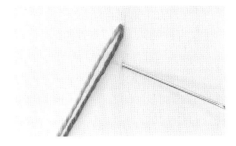

Step 1: Thread a needle with two lengths of thread in different colours and then work a single straight stitch.

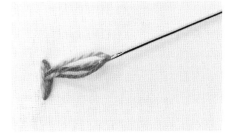

Step 2: Bring the needle back up through the centre of the stitch, between the two threads.

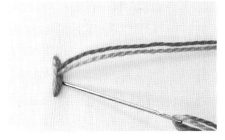

Step 3: Take the needle back into the fabric to the right, creating a small downward-slanting diagonal stitch.

Step 4: Work subsequent stitches in exactly the same way.

TIP Any type of embroidery thread can be used for this stitch, depending on the weight of the fabric and the effect you wish to create.

Leaf Stitch

Also known as Cretan leaf stitch or closed Cretan stitch, this can be worked as an open stitch, allowing the fabric to show through, or with the stitches placed closer together. The method of making the stitches is widely known as Cretan stitch (see page 35) but here, as the name implies, it is specifically used for embroidering leaf and petal shapes.

> ◀ *Using two strands of cotton embroidery thread throughout, leaf shapes are worked with small spaces in between, while those for the petals are placed more closely together, showing how the stitch can be varied for different effects. The stems are worked in stem stitch (see page 30).*

To work a leaf stitch:

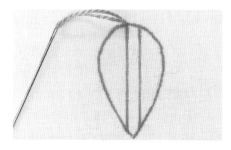

Step 1: Draw a leaf shape; add two lines down the centre of the shape. Bring the needle out at the top of the shape, at the top of one of the central lines, just outside the outline.

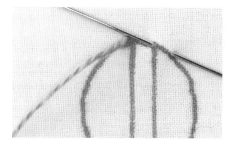

Step 2: Insert the needle on the opposite side, to form a slanted single straight stitch, then bring it back out at the top of the nearer of the central lines, with the thread below the needle.

Step 3: Now take the needle into the fabric on the other side of the outline and back out on the nearer central line, again with the thread below the needle.

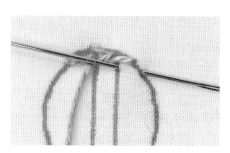

Step 4: Once again, take the needle into the fabric on the opposite side, as in step 2.

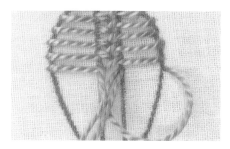

Step 5: Repeat the process, working from one side to the other, moving down the shape and leaving small gaps between the stitches or working the stitches closer together, as you prefer.

TIP You can alter the shape and size of the leaf – or petal – for this technique, as long as the overall shape remains quite simple. Any type of embroidery thread can be used for this stitch, depending on the weight of the fabric and the size of the leaf.

Cross Stitch

Though cross stitch is usually associated with counted-thread embroidery, it is also a useful surface embroidery stitch on any fabric. One of the oldest stitches in the history of embroidery – and sometimes referred to as sampler stitch or Berlin stitch – it can be used individually, arranged in rows or evenly spaced patterns, or to create shapes. It is also useful for creating lettering and monograms.

Cross stitch has been a traditional choice for monograms, used to identify household linens when they were sent to the laundry. Monograms can be simple or, like this one, more elaborate.

To work a single cross stitch:

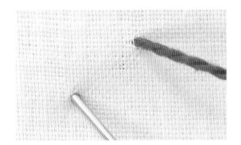

Step 1: To work a single cross stitch, bring the needle up through the fabric and take it down and to the left, then down into the fabric.

Step 2: Pull the thread taut to create a diagonal stitch, then bring it out directly above, level with the top of the first stitch.

Step 3: Take the needle across and into the fabric on the right, level with the base of the first stitch, and pull through to create a second diagonal that crosses the first.

To work a row of cross stitches:

Step 1: First, stitch the required number of single diagonal stitches, as in step 1.

Step 2: Come back along the row, this time making diagonal stitches in the other direction, forming a row of crosses.

TIP Whenever you work a number of cross stitches, whether they are in a row or separate, follow the basic rule that the top diagonal of each stitch should always face in the same direction.

Detached Chain

This stitch is traditionally used to form single petals that can be arranged to form a simple daisy motif – hence the nickname of 'lazy daisy' stitch. Make a variation – long-tailed daisy – by extending the length of the straight stitch that anchors the loop.

◄ *Using two strands of cotton embroidery thread, both leaves and flower petals have been worked in detached chain, with stem stitch (see page 30) for the stems and French knots (see page 80) for the flower centres.*

To work detached chain:

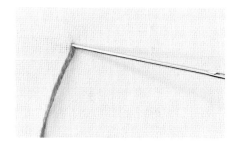

Step 1: Bring the needle up through the fabric and insert it again into the same place.

Step 2: Pull it through, creating a small loop of thread.

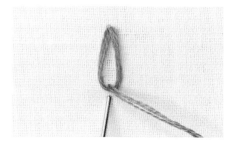

Step 3: Bring the tip of the needle up through the loop and pull it through, then re-insert it, trapping the loop in place with a small straight stitch.

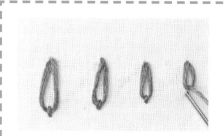

Variation 1: Vary the stitch by altering the size of the loop.

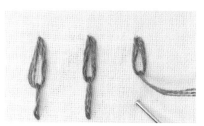

Variation 2: Vary it further by extending the length of the tying-down stitch.

Fishbone Stitch

Used to fill a medium-sized simple shape or worked between parallel lines to form a solid bar, the stitches overlapping in the centre form a plaited effect. This stitch is very useful for embroidering leaves, petals – and fish. When stitches are laid close together, a solid filling is formed, completely covering the fabric – but it can also be worked with gaps between the stitches, creating a more lacy effect known as open fishbone.

Stranded thread is a good choice for this stitch, as it lies nice and flat. Three strands have been used for this motif.

To work fishbone stitch:

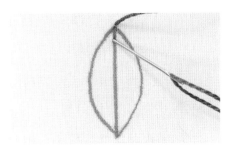

Step 1: Draw a shape and add a single line down the centre. Bring the needle up at the top of the shape and make a straight stitch, inserting the needle on the centre line.

Step 2: Bring the needle up on the left-hand side of the outline, just below the starting point, and back down just to the right of the first straight stitch.

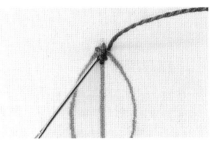

Step 3: Bring the needle up on the right-hand side of the outline, just below the starting point, over the second straight stitch, and back into the fabric right next to this second stitch.

Step 4: Now come out on the left-hand side of the outline again and back into the fabric over the third stitch.

Step 5: Each time, come out on the opposite outline and over the last stitch worked, moving down the shape.

Step 6: When the shape has been filled, take the thread to the wrong side and fasten off.

Tête De Boeuf

One of a small group of single stitches that can be used alone, as an accent, in evenly spaced ranks as a formal pattern, or scattered as an open filling, this makes a good companion to wheatear (page 56) and resembles a small flower bud.

◀ *Repeated in evenly spaced rows, using coton à broder, this motif forms a regular pattern – but it can look equally effective used less formally.*

To work tête de boeuf:

Step 1: Bring the needle up through the fabric where you want the top of the stitch to be, then re-insert it in the same place, leaving a loop of thread.

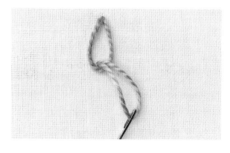

Step 2: Bring the needle up through the loop where you want the base of the stitch to be and pull the thread through.

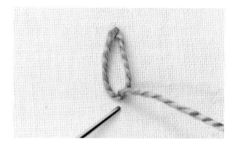

Step 3: Take the needle over the thread and into the fabric to secure the loop.

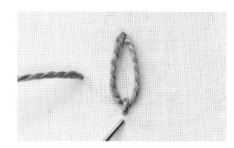

Step 4: Make a straight stitch on the left, slanting towards a point just below the base of the detached chain.

Step 5: Make a similar straight stitch on the right, slanting the other way.

Wrapped Cross Stitch

This stitch is three-dimensional and stands out, proud of the fabric. It is a good companion to bullion stitch (page 79), French knots (page 80) and corded bar (page 78), among others.

The small red crosses are made using three strands of cotton embroidery thread, while all the others – which are more prominent – are stitched using perle thread.

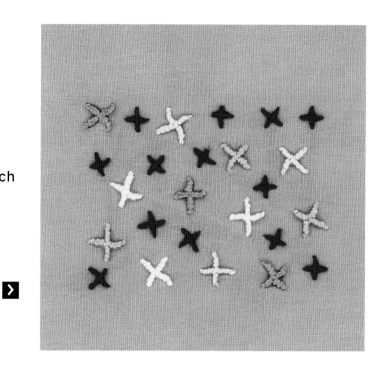

To work wrapped cross stitch:

Step 1: Make a medium-to-large cross stitch, then bring the needle up through the fabric at the end of the lower stitch.

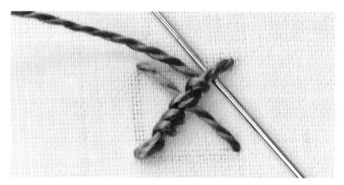

Step 2: Wrap the thread around the stitch by taking the needle under the thread several times, always in the same direction and without picking up the fabric.

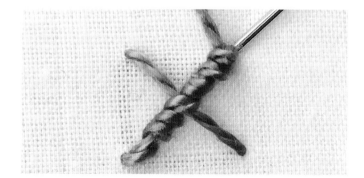

Step 3: Insert the needle into the fabric at the other end of the stitch.

Step 4: Repeat the process around the other stitch that forms the cross.

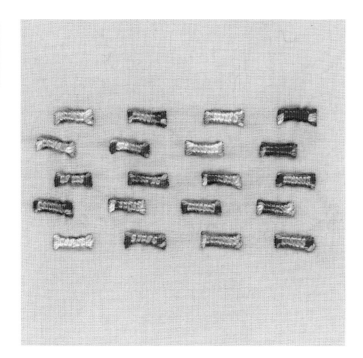

Corded Bar

Also known as a detached bar, this is another of a family of stitches that is formed above the surface of the ground fabric. This stitch is useful for making short, thick stems and other textured elements, such as seeds, insects, or even fence posts or small boats.

> ◀ *Perle thread is a good choice for this stitch, giving good texture and definition. Corded bars are best kept quite short and worked with the fabric in a hoop to minimise puckering.*

To work corded bar:

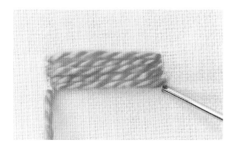

Step 1: Begin with a foundation of six surface satin stitches (see tip), all the same length.

Step 2: Bring the needle up through the fabric at one end of the stitches and take it under all six stitches, from top to bottom, without picking up the fabric. Use the blunt end of the needle.

Step 3: Take it under the stitches again, from top to bottom, making sure the loop of thread lies next to the first loop when you pull it taut.

Step 4: Continue whipping the thread around the foundation stitches, always in the same direction and pulling the thread taut each time, so that the stitches become tightly wrapped.

Step 5: When the foundation stitches are completely wrapped, take the needle back through the fabric, close to the end, and fasten off.

TIP Satin stitch (page 103) is worked by taking the needle under the fabric and starting each stitch on the same side each time. For surface satin stitch, used in step 1, take the needle out directly next to the point where it last went in. Long stitches are formed on the top of the fabric, as in regular satin stitch, but not on the wrong side.

Bullion Stitch

This long, coiled knot stitch is one of a family of stitches that includes French knots (page 80) and is useful for creating texture in an embroidered design. It is often used to form leaves and flowers – such as the bullion roses shown here.

Arrange three bullion stitches in a group to create a flower centre and place further stitches around the edge to form a rose, here stitched in a variegated perle thread. Single bullion stitches further enhance the design.

To work bullion stitch:

Step 1: Bring the needle up through the fabric, insert it a stitch length away and bring it back out at the point where it first emerged, leaving a loop of thread.

Step 2: Twist the needle around the thread between five and eight times.

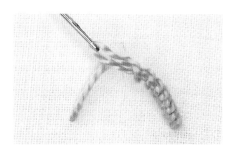

Step 3: Carefully pull the needle through the spiralling twists of thread to form the stitch.

Step 4: Re-insert the needle at the point where the thread emerges from the fabric.

Step 5: Pull the thread through until the coil of thread lies on the surface of the fabric.

TIP In step 3, hold the twists of thread in place with the forefinger of your non-dominant hand while you pull the needle through.

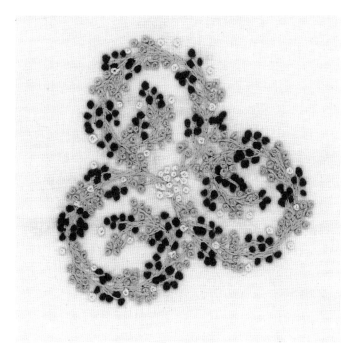

French Knot

French knots are a staple stitch. A single knot will add a tiny accent such as a dainty flower centre or an eye, while a scattering of French knots, whether widely spaced or tightly packed, adds a unique texture.

◀ *Here, French knots have been worked in clusters on a foundation of stems embroidered in split stitch. Two strands of cotton thread have been used throughout.*

To work a French knot:

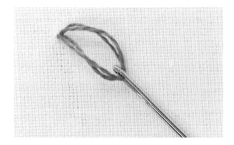

Step 1: Thread the needle with one or two strands of thread and bring it up through the fabric.

Step 2: Wind the tip of the needle twice around the thread, starting where it emerges from the fabric.

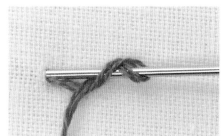

Step 3: Using a finger to hold the thread taut, insert the needle tip into the fabric close to where it emerged.

Step 4: Pull the needle down through the fabric, allowing it to pass down through the twists of thread, which will form a knot on the surface.

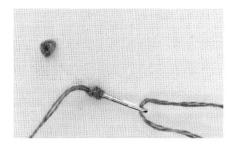

Step 5: If you are making more French knots nearby, simply take the thread across the back of the work to the new position. Otherwise, fasten off the thread neatly on the back of the work.

Four-legged Knot

This is a useful little stitch to add a small accent or to scatter over an area as a filling. It can also be worked in rows as a border or band. Any type of embroidery thread can be used.

Any thread can be used for this stitch, but a smooth thread such as perle gives good definition. Here it is used to create a border and for open filling – or seeding.

To work a four-legged knot:

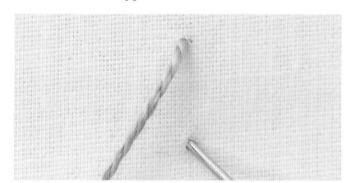

Step 1: Make a straight vertical stitch.

Step 2: Bring the needle out to the right, half a stitch length away. Take the thread across the vertical stitch, then take the needle under the stitch and over the loop of thread.

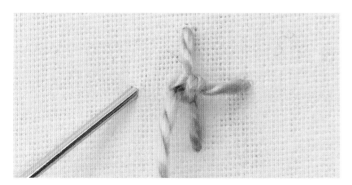

Step 3: Pull the thread to create a knot, then insert the needle to the left to create a horizontal bar, completing the cross.

Step 4: Pull the thread through and fasten off on the wrong side.

Woven Wheel

Worked by weaving thread in and out of a foundation of straight stitches arranged like the spokes of a wheel, this stitch – sometimes called woven spoke stitch or spider web – is easy to do and forms an attractive raised circle with plenty of scope for combining colours and thread textures.

◀ *Two strands of cotton thread have been used for all the foundation stitches. For the weaving, you can also try perle cotton and embroidery ribbon, which produce very different effects.*

To work woven wheel:

Step 1: Make an odd number of straight stitches – in this case, seven – of the same length, radiating out from a central point.

Step 2: Thread a blunt needle with the same or a contrasting thread and bring it up through the fabric, close to the centre.

Step 3: Working either clockwise or anti-clockwise, whichever is easier, take the needle over the first 'spoke' and under the next.

Step 4: Continue in the same direction, taking the needle alternately over and under each straight stitch.

Step 5: Continue until you reach the outer limit of the spokes then take the needle through the fabric, close to the edge of the circle, and fasten off.

Step 6: To finish, take the needle through the fabric, close to the edge of the circle, and fasten off.

Whipped Wheel

Forming a circular shape with raised ribs, this motif, also known as ribbed wheel and back-stitched spider's web, can be used as an accent, a flower centre, a wheel hub – all kinds of creative applications. Experiment with different-coloured threads for an attractive effect.

Three strands of cotton thread have been used here for both the foundation stitches and the whipped thread. You can see that both plain and variegated threads produce pretty effects.

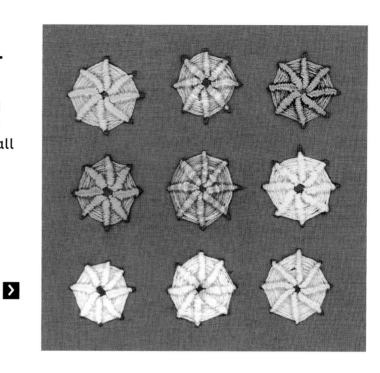

To work whipped wheel:

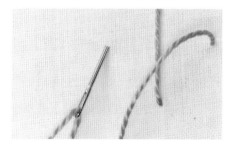

Step 1: Stitch the foundation, creating an even number of 'spokes' radiating from a central point. Start with two straight stitches overlapping to form an upright cross.

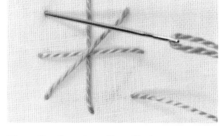

Step 2: Overlay the first cross with another one formed of two diagonal stitches, to create eight spokes.

Step 3: Thread a blunt needle with a second thread and bring the needle up close to the centre, where the foundation stitches intersect. Pass it under the nearest stitch or spoke.

Step 4: Pass the needle back over the last stitch, then forwards under two stitches.

Step 5: Carry on like this, each time passing back over one thread and forwards under two.

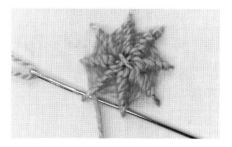

Step 6: Continue until all the spokes are filled and the wheel will be complete.

Raised Cup

Worked on a base of three straight stitches, using a twisted buttonhole stitch, this creates a small raised circle, like a bud, that is the perfect partner for other raised stitches such as French knots (page 80) and bullion stitch (page 79) in a textured embroidery design.

◀ *The little cups resemble flower buds, effective here arranged in a loose cluster. Detached chain stitches in green complete the motif.*

To work a raised cup:

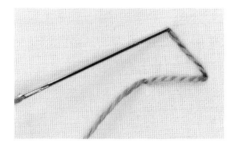

Step 1: Make a foundation of three backstitches arranged in a triangular formation.

Step 2: Bring the needle up at one corner. Take it under the first backstitch and under the working thread, then over the thread.

Step 3: Pull the needle through so that a knot forms around the threads.

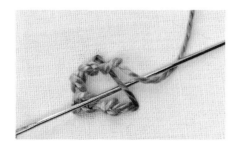

Step 4: Make another knot in the same way, then make two knots on each of the other two back-stitches.

Step 5: For the second round, which sits on top of the first, take the needle under the thread between the next two knotted stitches and make another knot in the same way as before.

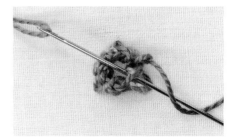

Step 6: Repeat step 5 five times more, each time taking the needle under the thread between the knotted stitches of the previous round. To finish, insert the needle down into the centre of the cup.

God's Eye

Similar in construction to a whipped wheel (page 83), this motif is worked on a foundation of two intersecting straight stitches, forming a diamond shape on a stalk.

By positioning four individual god's eyes in a cluster, with French knots in the centre, an attractive formal cross motif is formed.

To work a God's eye:

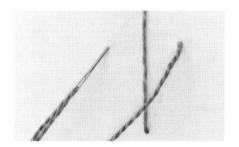

Step 1: Start with the foundation: make two stitches, one of them a vertical straight stitch and the other a shorter straight stitch across it, just above the centre.

Step 2: Thread a blunt needle with a contrasting thread and bring it up close to the intersection of the cross.

Step 3: Take the needle diagonally across the intersection, then from right to left under the next two threads.

Step 4: Take the needle back over the last thread, then under that thread and the next.

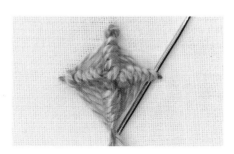

Step 5: Repeat this process – back one thread and forward two – until the space has been filled.

Woven Picot

This raised petal-shaped stitch can be used to add texture and a three-dimensional element to lots of different designs, or repeated at intervals as a decorative edging to a hem.

Six woven picots worked in coton à broder are arranged to make the petals of a 3D flower. You could work five instead, to make a starfish.

To work a woven picot:

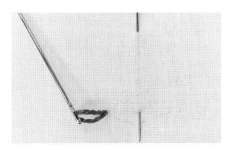

Step 1: Mark the length of the finished stitch by inserting a pin into the fabric. Bring the needle out of the fabric to the left of the pin, level with the base point.

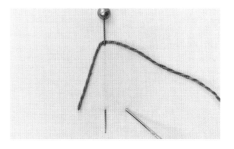

Step 2: Take the thread around the head of the pin and insert the needle on the opposite side.

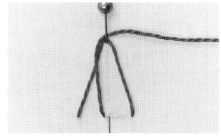

Step 3: Bring the needle back out close to the point of the pin and take the thread around the head of the pin again.

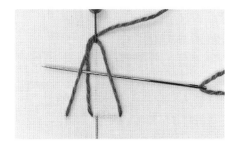

Step 4: Now begin weaving: take the needle under the right-hand thread, over the centre thread and under the left-hand thread.

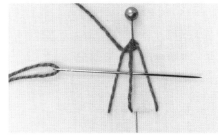

Step 5: Working in the other direction, from left to right, take the needle over the left-hand thread, under the centre thread and over the right-hand thread.

Step 6: Repeat steps 4 and 5 until you reach the base, then take the needle down through the base of the right-hand thread to complete the picot.

Raised Knot

With a simple embellishment, a line of plain running stitch is transformed into a solid line with a twisted appearance, like a cord. Use the same thread for both operations or, better still, for the whipping use a thread of similar weight but a different colour, or a different type of thread for a textural contrast.

Whipped running stitch makes an attractive outline for this butterfly motif. Four strands of floss are used for this, for the French knots on the antennae, and for the satin-stitched body and head.

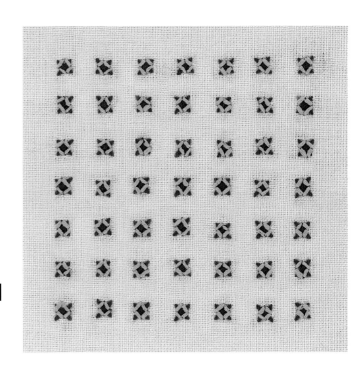

To work a raised knot:

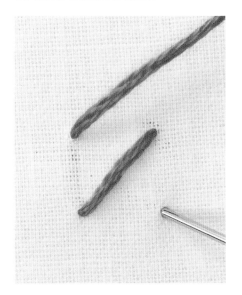

Step 1: Work a single cross stitch (page 73).

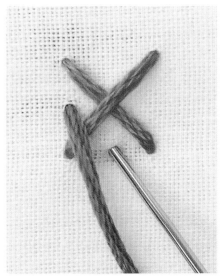

Step 2: With the same or a contrast thread, work a straight stitch over one of the arms of the cross.

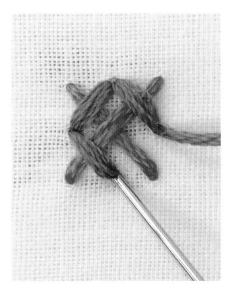

Step 3: Now work a straight stitch over each of the other arms of the cross, with the ends of the stitches joined, like backstitch.

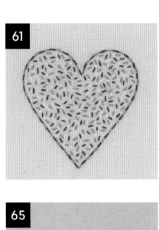

61

62

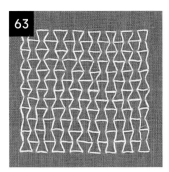

63

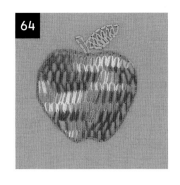

64

65

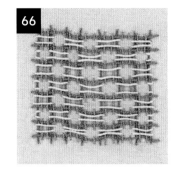

66

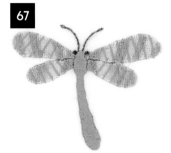

67

68

69

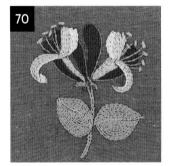

70

71

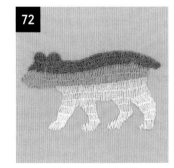

72

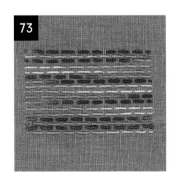

73

74

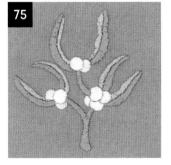

75

76

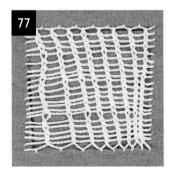

77

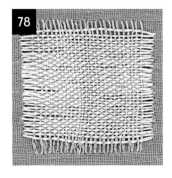

78

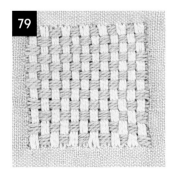

79

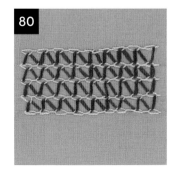

80

Filling Stitches

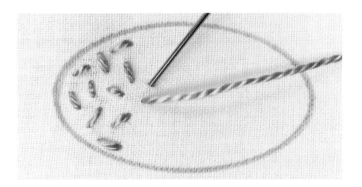

Seed Stitch

This open filling stitch is easy to work but success depends on even distribution. That said, seed stitches can be arranged close together or further apart, depending on the effect you wish to achieve. Tightly packed seed stitches can also be used as a foundation for padded satin stitch (see page 104). Other names for this stitch include isolated backstitch and speckling stitch. Another version (shown below) is dot stitch.

◀ *Confetti-like seed stitches are ideal for filling a simple shape such as this heart, which is outlined with Holbein stitch (see page 40) for a harmonious partnership.*

To work seed stitch:

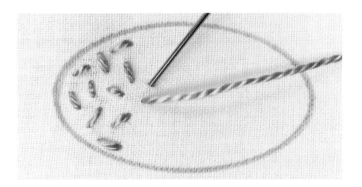

Step 1: Mark the area to be filled. Make a small, straight stitch by bringing the needle up through the fabric and taking it back down a small distance away. Fill the area by working individual seed stitches of approximately the same length, evenly spaced and pointing in different directions.

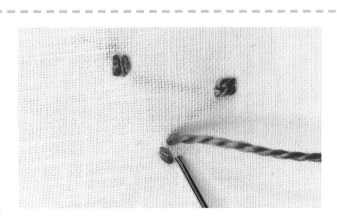

Dot stitch: Another version of seed stitch, sometimes known as dot stitch, is formed of two adjacent stitches. Make a single seed stitch, as described in step 1, then make a second stitch immediately next to it.

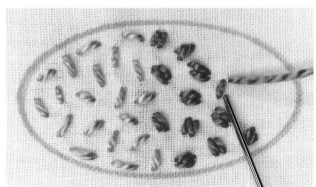

Spacing options: Seed stitches, either the single or double version, or both, can be spaced far apart or close together, for different effects.

Fly Stitch Filling

Related to fly stitch (see page 70), this employs rows of evenly sized stitches to form an open honeycomb or trellis pattern that can be used to fill regular-shaped areas of any size. Stitches can also be arranged in vertical or horizontal lines, for a zigzag or chevron effect.

The arrangement of stitches, in vertical lines forming a chevron pattern and worked in two strands of cotton embroidery thread, follows the subtle curves of the wing and tail, and is combined with scattered individual fly stitches on the body. The overall shape is outlined in Holbein stitch (see page 40), using two shades of blue thread.

To work fly stitch filling:

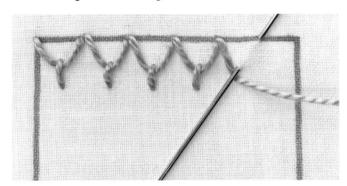

Step 1: Draw the shape to be filled. Work a horizontal row of fly stitches (see page 70) with short tails along the top row, with the tips of the diagonal stitches touching.

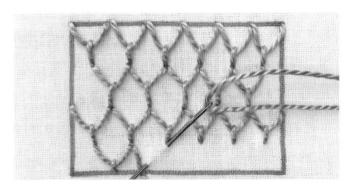

Step 2: Work second and subsequent rows in the same way, forming an even pattern.

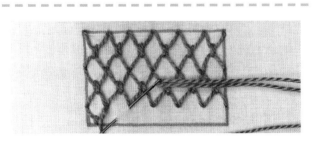

Diamond trellis effect: Work the first row as shown in step 1. Work the following and alternate rows with the stitches inverted and the tails placed next to the tails of the previous row.

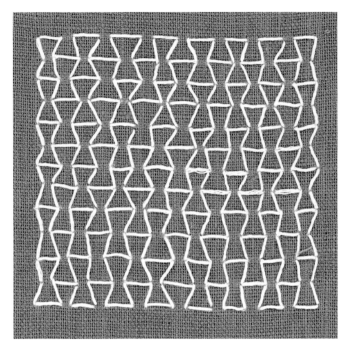

Japanese Darning Stitch

This variation of running stitch, is a light, open filling stitch suitable for most fabrics. It produces an attractive geometric mesh pattern and can be used to fill most simple shapes of almost any size.

◄ *A variegated perle thread has been used here on a fabric with a visible weave to help maintain even rows of stitching.*

To work Japanese darning stitch:

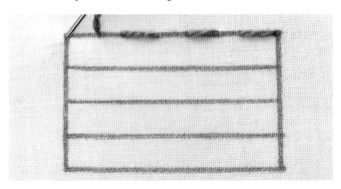

Step 1: Work the first row from right to left. Draw the shape to be filled, divide it by evenly spaced horizontal lines and work a row of running stitches, making the gaps between them shorter than the stitches.

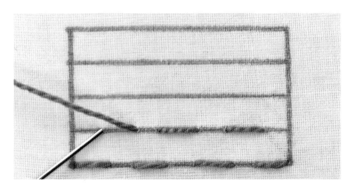

Step 2: Turn the work, to enable you to work the next row from right to left. Work a second row of running stitch, similar to the first, staggering the stitches as shown.

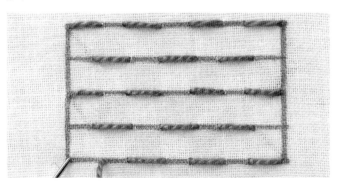

Step 3: Turning the work at the end of each row, as before, work several more rows of running stitch. The rows will form a pattern similar to brick stitch (see page 102).

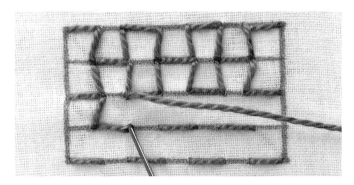

Step 4: Join the ends of stitches on one row with those in the row below, to create an ordered pattern.

Wave Filling

This woven stitch, also known as looped shading, produces a lacy effect that can be altered by changing the spacing of the stitches. Use a single colour, or change colours every row or every few rows for a shaded effect.

Simple shapes like this apple are easiest to work with. Three strands of variegated thread have been used, with plain green for the leaf, and the shapes have been outlined in backstitch (see page 27).

To work wave filling:

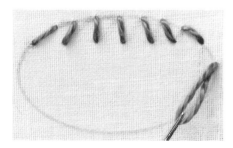

Step 1: Draw the shape to be filled and work a row of vertical straight stitches, from left to right, along the top. Bring the needle up through the fabric on the right-hand side, a little way below.

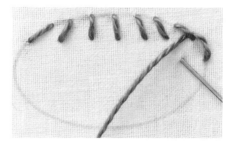

Step 2: Take the needle under the stitch above, from right to left, then back into the fabric below.

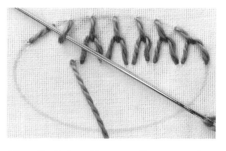

Step 3: Bring the needle up to the left, adjacent to where it just went in, and repeat step 2. Repeat to the end of the row.

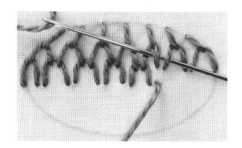

Step 4: Bring the needle up through the fabric a little way below. Now work across the row in a similar way but taking the needle under two threads, from left to right.

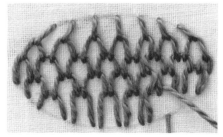

Step 5: Continue working downwards in rows, back and forth, taking the needle under two threads, until the shape has been filled.

Cloud Filling

This stitch, also known as Mexican stitch, involves weaving a thread through a foundation of short, evenly spaced stitches. It can be effective when worked in the same thread throughout or with two threads of contrasting colour or weight, and is useful for filling simple shapes on either plain or even-weave fabric. The effect is like a kind of diamond lattice or trellis.

◄ *This cloud shape uses two strands of white embroidery thread for both the foundation stitches and the lacing. The whole shape is then outlined with backstitch (see page 27).*

To work cloud filling stitch:

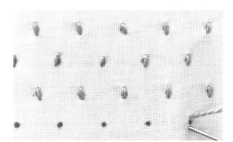

Step 1: Mark rows of dots, evenly spaced, on the area of fabric to be filled. On each dot, stitch a short upright straight stitch. This forms the foundation.

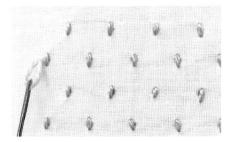

Step 2: Thread a blunt needle with the same or a contrast thread. Bring the needle up through the fabric adjacent to the first stitch on the left-hand side of the second row down.

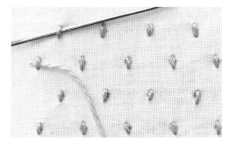

Step 3: Take the needle under the stitch from left to right, then under the stitch above, from left to right.

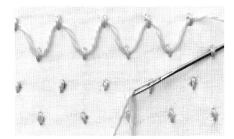

Step 4: Repeat step 3 to the end of the row, then insert the needle into the fabric adjacent to the last stitch.

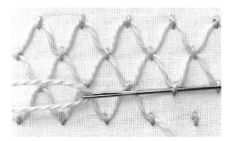

Step 5: Bring the thread up in the next starting place, which in this case is the same stitch. Now, working from right to left, repeat the process until the whole foundation has been covered.

TIP You can work from the bottom upwards, rather than from the top downwards, if you find this easier.

Plaid Filling

This is a form of couching, where a regular pattern of criss-crossed threads resembles a plaid or tartan fabric. Usually worked in three colours, it is relatively easy to do and useful for filling areas of various sizes and regular shapes.

This is quite a specific stitch, with little scope for variation, but you can enjoy choosing attractive colour combinations. Here, perle thread has been used, giving a good definition to the pattern.

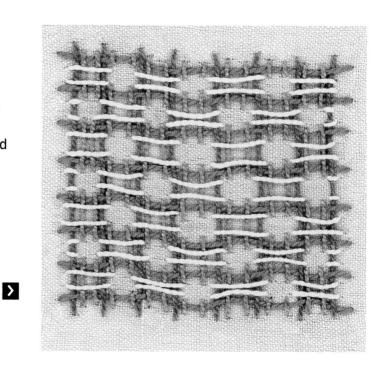

To work plaid filling stitch:

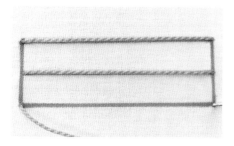

Step 1: Draw the shape to be filled, with some horizontal guidelines across if necessary. Work long horizontal stitches across the shape.

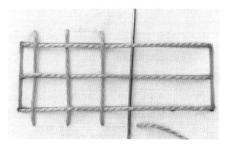

Step 2: Work vertical stitches, alternating between taking the needle under and over the horizontal stitches at the points where they intersect. You need an even number of vertical stitches.

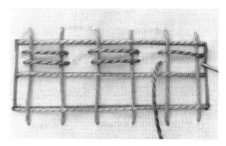

Step 3: With a second colour, sew a pair of horizontal parallel stitches across the squares, offsetting the stitches on subsequent rows.

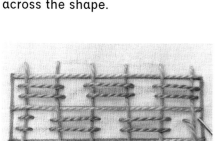

Step 4: On alternate rows, to create the offset pattern of horizontals, work shorter stitches across the single threads at the row ends.

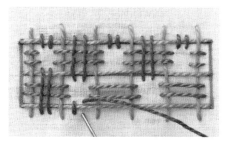

Step 5: With a third colour, work pairs of parallel vertical stitches over the centre of the horizontal line of each square, swapping short and long stitches along the rows and from one row to the next.

TIP If you prefer, you can work vertical stitches in step 3 and horizontal stitches in step 5, depending on the overall effect you wish to achieve.

Whipped Satin Stitch

An excellent choice for filling long, narrow shapes, this attractive variation of satin stitch produces a rich striped effect. The two layers of stitches can be worked in the same colour or using two contrasting colours.

◄ *This motif has a body and head worked in plain satin stitch (see page 103) and wings worked in whipped satin stitch, using a pretty variegated thread for the foundation layer.*

To work whipped satin stitch:

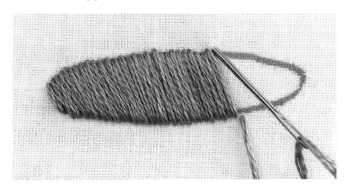

Step 1: Draw the design, making sure that each section to be filled is not too wide. Fill the shape with satin stitch (see page 103), worked at a slant.

Step 2: Thread the needle with a second thread in the same or a contrasting colour. Bring it up near one end of the shape.

Step 3: Work whipping stitches across the filled shape, with small gaps in between, and at a diagonal that crosses the foundation layer of slanting satin stitches.

TIP Be sure to work this stitch with the fabric stretched out taut in a hoop, to prevent puckering.

Basket Filling

Producing a flat, even basketweave pattern, this stitch, also known as basket satin stitch, can be used on either plain or even-weave fabric. It can be found in Jacobean embroidery but also has its uses in modern designs. Traditionally, it was worked in a single colour, but you can produce some interesting effects by introducing other colours; using two colours for alternate blocks would create a chequerboard effect.

An ideal use for this stitch is to embroider a basket. Here, it has been used to good effect on the main body of the basket and to create a curved handle. ▶

To work basket filling:

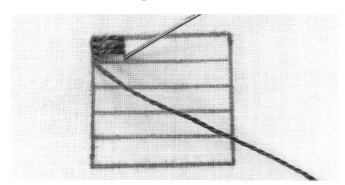

Step 1: Draw the shape to be filled and mark a series of lines as a guide to the rows of stitch blocks, to help produce an even result. Work four horizontal satin stitches (see page 103) within the lines.

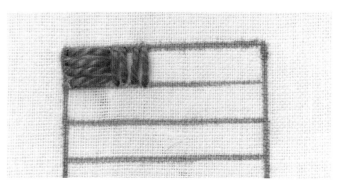

Step 2: Now work four vertical stitches adjacent to the first set and of a similar length. Make sure the stitches are placed closely together.

Step 3: Continue along the line, alternating horizontal and vertical stitch blocks.

Step 4: Continue in this way, making sure each set of stitches lies in a different direction to the one next to it.

Split Stitch Shading

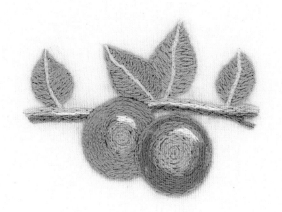

Split stitch proves its versatility when used to fill shapes. You can alter the stitch length, change colours when required, and work the rows of stitches to follow quite intricate shapes and contours. This works best with stranded threads.

◄ *Worked in multiple rows, closely spaced, using two strands of cotton thread, split stitch follows the contours of the various shapes and allows for an excellent degree of fine detail.*

To work split stitch shading:

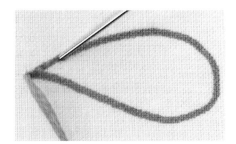

Step 1: Draw the shape to be filled. Working from left to right, bring the needle up on the outline, then take it down a stitch length to the right.

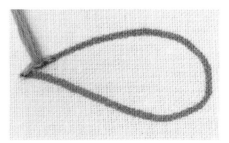

Step 2: Pull the thread through to form the first stitch, then bring the needle back up through the centre of the stitch.

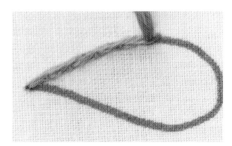

Step 3: Repeat this along the length of the line.

Step 4: Working from right to left – or turning the work to work from left to right – make another line of split stitch close to the first, offsetting the stitches so that the centres and ends do not line up.

Step 5: Change colours where appropriate, to form subtle gradations of colour.

Stem Stitch Shading

Working stem stitch in close rows, you can achieve a solid, close-woven effect that is suitable for almost any shape, such as fruit, flowers, foliage and illustrative motifs. Any type of embroidery thread can be used.

This honeysuckle design shows that even quite intricate shapes can be filled with stem stitch, and colours can be changed for subtle shading effects. Two strands of cotton thread are used here, with a single strand for the fine filaments.

To work stem stitch shading:

Step 1: Draw the shape to be filled. Embroider a line of stem stitch along one edge, from left to right, covering the drawn line. Try to keep the stitches even and consistent in length.

Step 2: Start the next row on the left, immediately below the previous row. You may have to make the first stitch slightly shorter so that stitches fit snugly against the previous row.

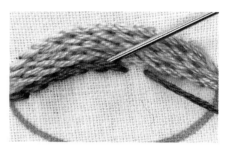

Step 3: Change colours where necessary, to create a shaded effect. This can be subtle or bold.

Step 4: The stitch lines should follow the contours of the shape. Aim to make stitches consistent in length, but you may need to make some shorter or longer around a curve or at the end of a line.

TIP You can choose to work each stitch in a single movement, pushing the needle in and out again, as in step 1, or use a stabbing motion (see page 18), as in steps 2, 3 and 4.

Buttonhole Shading

By working close-packed rows of buttonhole or blanket stitch (see page 42 and 41), you can fill a shape with solid colour or a more openwork effect – and if you change colours at intervals, you can achieve a shaded effect. The stitches shown here are arranged in pairs, but you could use single stitches or groups of three or four for a different effect.

◀ *Rows of blanket stitches create an attractive filling. The wheels are filled using regular blanket stitch and the whole shape is outlined in backstitch.*

To work buttonhole shading:

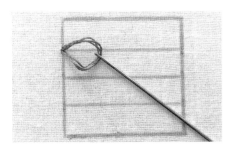

Step 1: Draw the shape to be filled and draw lines across it to divide it into strips. Bring the needle up through the fabric on the first of these lines.

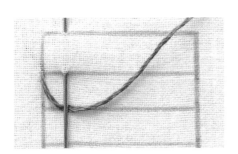

Step 2: Take the needle into the fabric on the outline above, then bring it back up on the line below, with the loop of thread under the tip of the needle, creating the first blanket stitch.

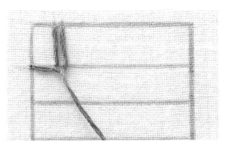

Step 3: Make another blanket stitch, close to the first.

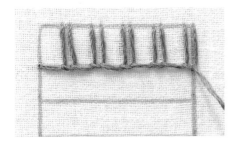

Step 4: Working from left to right, make further pairs of blanket stitches, evenly spaced.

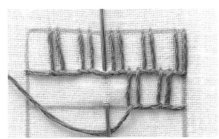

Step 5: For the second row, work from right to left and position the 'legs' of the blanket stitches over the bars of the previous row.

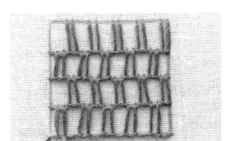

Step 6: As you work each row, it will be offset from the previous one, creating a kind of brickwork effect. Finish by taking the needle down into the fabric.

Plate Stitch

A good alternative to satin stitch (see page 103) or long and short stitch (see page 105) where larger areas need to be filled, this stitch produces an attractive close texture and allows you to change colour at intervals for a variegated effect.

Using two strands of cotton thread to fill a simple shape, colours are changed after each double row of stitches, producing a subtle shaded effect.

To work plate stitch:

Step 1: Draw the shape to be filled. Bring the needle up through the fabric at the top left and make a vertical stitch.

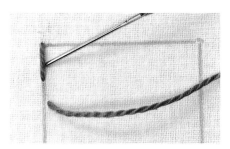

Step 2: Bring the needle back up a short distance below and then take it down just next to the first stitch, just below the centre of the stitch.

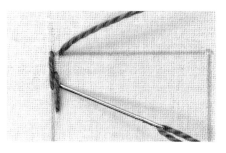

Step 3: Now make a stitch level with the first stitch and close to the previous one.

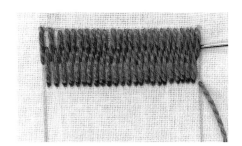

Step 4: Repeat this process across the width of the shape, so that you have completed a double row of stitches, closely spaced.

Step 5: Now make another double row, placing the stitches directly below the first set and inserting the needle between the stitches of the row above.

Step 6: Continue until the shape has been filled. On the last row, you may have to adjust the length of the stitches to fit the shape.

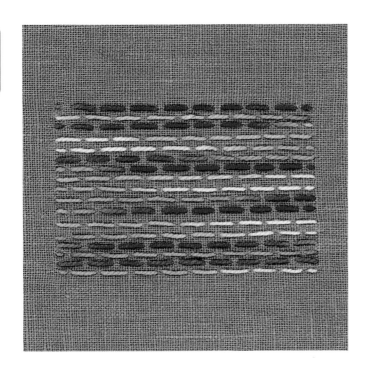

Brick Stitch

This belongs to the running stitch family, with stitches worked in formal rows to form a pattern reminiscent of a brick wall. It is easy to do – especially on a fabric with a clearly visible even weave – and can form an open or a closed effect, depending on the size of the gaps between the stitches and the rows.

Worked horizontally, this stitch can be used effectively to depict a brick wall. In this case, a variegated perle thread helps to create this effect.

To work brick stitch:

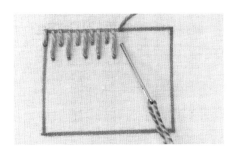

Step 1: Draw the shape for filling. Bring the needle up in the top left and work a foundation row of alternate long and short vertical stitches, bringing the needle out on the top line each time.

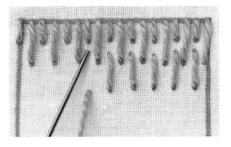

Step 2: Work vertical stitches of equal length (the same as the first row) lining up each one with one of the short stitches above. There should be a small gap between the ends of the stitches.

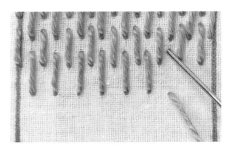

Step 3: For the next and subsequent rows, work stitches of the same length in between the stitches of the previous row.

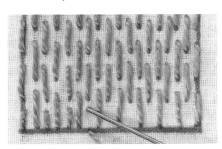

Step 4: For the last row, you will need to work shorter stitches to fill the shape and line up with the lower guideline.

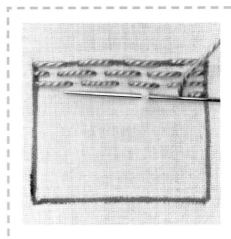

Horizontal variation: An alternative is to make parallel rows of running stitch, with the stitches equal in length and small spaces in between. The rows should be offset, with the ends of stitches in one row level with the centres of the stitches in the rows above and below. You will need to make half-length stitches at either end of alternate rows.

Satin Stitch

Satin stitch, also known as flat satin stitch or damask stitch, is the perfect way to cover small areas and shapes with a solid colour. The stitches should be close together and parallel, with no gaps between them, in order to create this solid effect. Stitches should also be kept quite short so that they do not snag or pull, so make sure that the shapes to be filled are quite small. For larger shapes, it is advisable to use another solid filling such as long and short stitch (see page 105).

This rose motif is an ideal subject for satin stitch, as both the flower and the leaves are made up of lots of small shapes.

To work satin stitch:

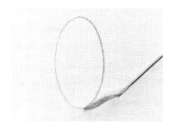

Step 1: Draw the outline of the shape to be filled and bring the needle out at the base of the shape on the right-hand side of the outline.

Step 2: Take the needle down into the fabric on the left-hand side of the outline. Pull the thread through.

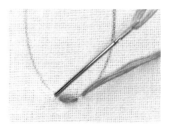

Step 3: Bring the needle back out on the right-hand side, next to the first stitch. Work upwards and keep the stitches close together.

Step 4: If you run out of thread halfway through, take the needle to the wrong side of the work and pass the needle under the stitches.

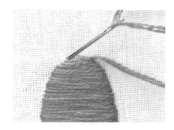

Step 5: When you reach the top of the shape, take the needle to the wrong side and fasten off the thread as described in step 4.

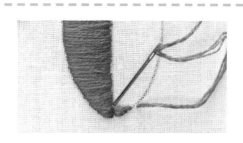

Larger shapes: Divide into smaller areas and start with the left-hand section. Fill in the other side, very close to the ends of the first stitches.

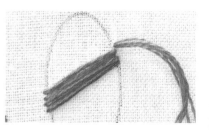

Slanted variation: It can be easier to start in the centre and work outwards, in two stages. This can help keep the stitches parallel.

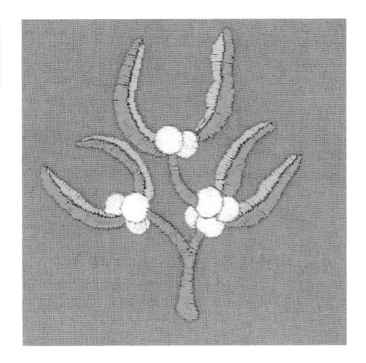

Padded Satin Stitch

A simple variation of basic satin stitch (see page 103), this version ensures good coverage, with no fabric show-through, and a rich, padded effect. It is best used to cover small areas. If you have a large area to fill, divide it into smaller shapes to ensure that stitches are not too long and liable to snag.

◀ *Each part of this design is relatively small, so stitches can be kept short. For the leaves, running stitch provides the padding, while berries are worked in layers of satin stitch.*

To work padded satin stitch:

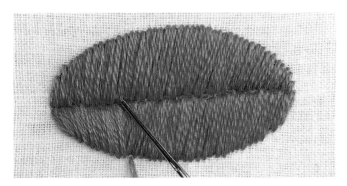

Step 1: Draw the outline of the shape to be filled. Fill the shape with lines of running stitch, with small gaps between the stitches to ensure good coverage.

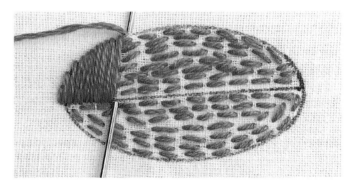

Step 2: Now use satin stitch to fill the shapes, making sure that stitches lie close together, to cover the foundation stitches.

Step 3: For an enhanced padded effect, work another layer of satin stitch on top of the first, with the stitches lying in a different direction.

TIP As the foundation stitches are simply there to act as padding and will be covered, you can use up spare bits of thread for this purpose – though it is a good idea to choose colours similar to those used for the top layer of satin stitch.

Long and Short Stitch

An excellent alternative to satin stitch (page 103) when you need to fill a larger shape, the inner rows of stitches produce irregular joins that allow subtle colour changes that can be used to create graduated blends and shaded effects. Other names for this stitch are embroidery stitch, shading stitch, Irish stitch and plumage stitch.

This stitch is ideal for 'painting' with thread and this is shown to good effect in this pansy design using two strands of cotton thread.

To work long and short stitch:

Step 1: Draw the outline of the shape to be filled. Bring the needle up on the outline and work a short stitch and then a long one, placing the stitches close together.

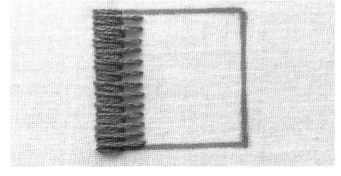

Step 2: Work the first row with alternating long and short stitches, so that the fabric is completely covered, with no gaps between stitches.

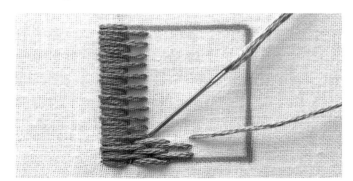

Step 3: For the second and subsequent rows, work stitches of equal length. As you make each stitch, insert the needle into the same place as the end of the corresponding stitch on the previous row.

Step 4: For the last row, as you follow the edge of the shape, the stitches will be long and short, as in the first row.

Ceylon Stitch

Similar in appearance to knitted stocking stitch – and sometimes called knitted stitch or Peruvian knitting – this open filling can be used for most shapes. The stitches can be worked close together or further apart, for different effects.

◀ *Perle thread, being smooth, shows the structure of this stitch to good advantage. You can clearly see the resemblance to a knitted fabric.*

To work Ceylon stitch:

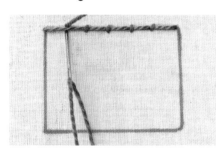

Step 1: Draw a shape for filling. Bring the needle up top left and down at top right, making a long stitch. From right to left, make a series of small vertical stitches worked across at regular intervals.

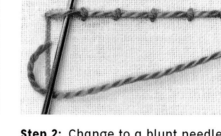

Step 2: Change to a blunt needle and bring it up through the fabric below the starting point. Pass the needle under the top thread from top to bottom, with the thread beneath the needle.

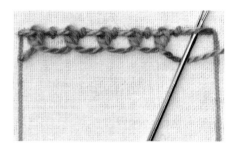

Step 3: Repeat this process along the row, then insert the needle into the guideline.

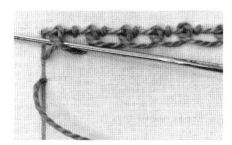

Step 4: Carry the needle across the back and bring it out again on the left, a little way down. Pass it from right to left under two strands of the loop above, without piercing the fabric. Repeat along the line.

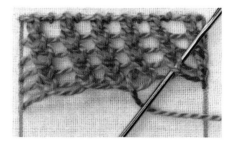

Step 5: Repeat step 4 until the shape has been filled.

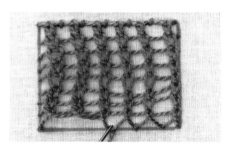

Step 6: Change back to an embroidery needle and fasten each loop of the last row to the fabric with a small vertical stitch.

Surface Darning

Traditionally used to mend holes in clothing and household linens, this stitch technique, sometimes referred to as needle weaving, can also be used to produce small, solid areas in embroidered designs. Use a single colour for both horizontal and vertical threads, or two contrasting shades.

This sample has been made using coton à broder on linen fabric. The visible weave of the fabric is useful as it provides guidelines to help produce a neat result. Meanwhile, the smooth thread makes weaving easier.

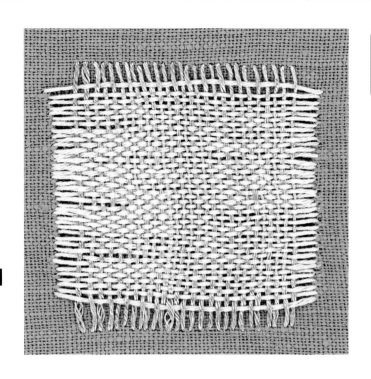

To work surface darning:

Step 1: Work a series of vertical satin stitches, close together and covering the area to be filled.

Step 2: Using a blunt needle, bring the needle up through the fabric close to one upper corner, and weave the needle under and over alternate vertical threads.

Step 3: When you reach the other side, take the needle down through the fabric and bring it back up immediately below.

Step 4: Weave the needle across to the other side, again alternating threads.

Step 5: Repeat this process, going back and forth from one side to the other.

TIP Stretch the fabric in an embroidery hoop. This will help to stop puckering; it also allows you to turn the work at the end of each row of weaving, enabling you to push the needle from right to left if you are right-handed, or from left to right if you are left-handed. This also applies to chequerboard darning (see page 108).

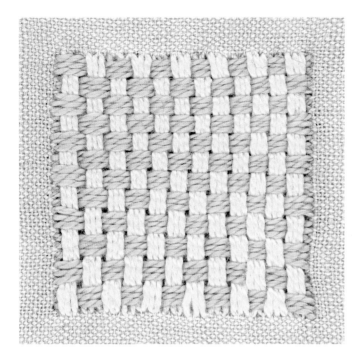

Chequerboard Darning

A variation of surface darning, sometimes known as plaited stitch, this stitch can be used for small areas and produces an attractive chequerboard pattern when two contrasting-coloured threads are used. It is best worked using a smooth thread and a blunt needle.

◀ *Perle thread is a good choice for this stitch as it is firm and smooth, making it easier to weave the needle over and under the strands, and produces good stitch definition.*

To work chequerboard darning:

Step 1: Work a foundation of vertical surface satin stitches over the area to be covered, making sure the stitches are placed close together. You need a multiple of three vertical threads.

Step 2: Bring a second thread up through the fabric near one corner. Take the needle over the first three threads and under the next three, alternating across the width. Take the needle down through the fabric.

Step 3: Bring the needle up again just below and go back across in the same pattern – under and over three threads at a time.

Step 4: Work a third row in the same way.

Step 5: Now work three more rows, going over the threads that you went under in rows 1–3 and vice versa.

Step 6: Continue like this, changing the sequence after every three rows.

Interlaced Cable Chain

Suitable for filling simple geometric shapes, this intricate stitch is very decorative, whether worked in a single colour or two or more contrasting shades. It is a variation of cable stitch.

Here, the cable stitch is worked in coton à broder and the lacing in a shiny stranded thread. A bold choice of colours displays this combination stitch to good advantage, showing that it can be effective as a decorative filling and also as a border or frame.

To work interlaced cable chain:

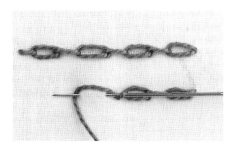

Step 1: Work two or more parallel rows of cable stitch (page 31), with the stitches lined up. Work with the rows arranged vertically.

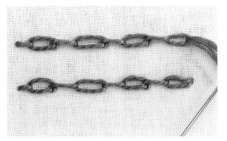

Step 2: Using the same or a contrasting thread, bring the needle up inside the first chain stitch at the top left.

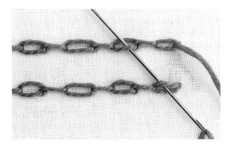

Step 3: Take the needle under the left-hand thread of the chain stitch on the next row, from right to left, and under the right-hand thread of the next chain stitch down on the left.

Step 4: Repeat step 3, taking the needle under the left-hand thread of the adjacent stitch to the right and under the right-hand thread of the next stitch down on the left.

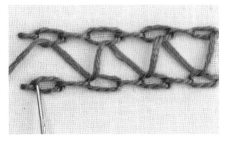

Step 5: Continue to the bottom of the two rows. Finish by taking the needle down inside the last chain on the right.

TIP If you are working with more than two lines of cable stitch, start the next line of zigzag interlacing by bringing the needle up inside the top chain of the next row to the right and repeating the process described above.

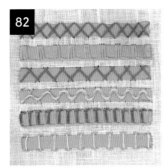

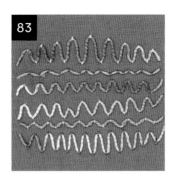

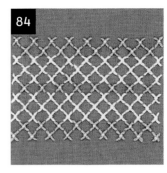

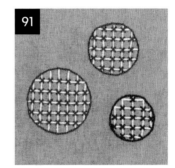

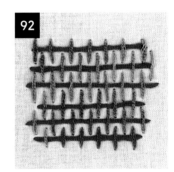

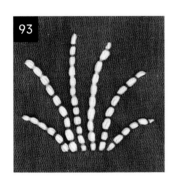

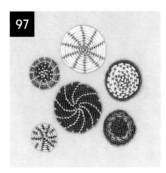

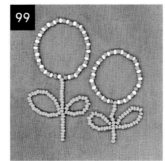

Couching and Laid Work

Couched Thread

The basic couching method, sometimes called Kloster stitch or convent stitch, produces a neat line. It is used to apply one or more threads to the surface of a fabric where the thread itself is too thick, too precious, too fragile or too highly textured to stitch into the fabric: instead, it is laid on the surface and held in place – or couched – with finer thread. The French word *coucher* means 'to lay down'.

◄ *This organic, tree-like design shows how the basic couching method can be used to lay single or multiple strands on the surface of a fabric to describe quite detailed forms.*

To work couched thread:

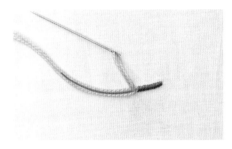

Step 1: Work from right to left. Bring the needle with the thread to be couched up through the fabric at the beginning of the line to be covered and hold the thread in place along the line.

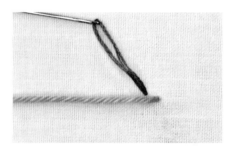

Step 2: Bring a second needle, with a finer thread – such as one or more strands of six-stranded cotton embroidery thread – up at the start of the line, adjacent to the thicker thread.

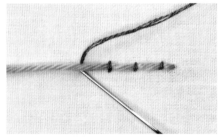

Step 3: Make a series of small stitches across the thicker thread, to tie it in place along the line.

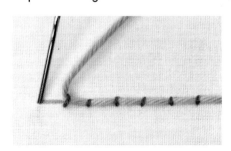

Step 4: At the end of the line, take the needle with the thicker thread down through the fabric.

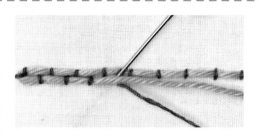

To create a wider line: Turn the laid thread and lay it alongside the first line, once again couching it with the finer thread, using small stitches.

TIP When working around a corner or tight curve, you may need to alter the spacing of the couching stitches, arranging them more closely together.

Fancy Couching

One step on from basic couching, this creates a more decorative or patterned effect. You can use a heavier thread, a double thread, or a narrow ribbon or braid, laid on the surface of the fabric, and any thread you wish for the couching. The tying stitches are worked through the fabric and over the laid threads. Many different stitches are suitable for this, so try the stitches shown here as well as others

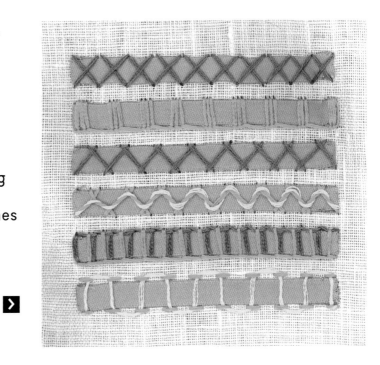

Here are some examples of different fancy couching stitches worked with three strands of cotton embroidery thread over lengths of ribbon.

To work fancy couching:

Step 1: Lay the thread or material to be couched across the surface of the fabric. Use a pin to hold one end in place. Bring the needle with the couching thread up through the fabric, close to one end.

Step 3: When you reach the end of the ribbon, take the needle down through the fabric and fasten off on the wrong side.

Step 2: Work the chosen stitch over the ribbon. In this case, the stitch is blanket stitch. Make sure, when working the stitches, that the needle does not pierce the ribbon.

TIP When couching ribbon or braid, you may need to neaten the cut ends. When couching threads, however, you may be able to finish the ends on the wrong side of the fabric.

Zigzag Couching

This stitch forms a narrow decorative band, useful for edging or framing an area and suitable for describing both straight lines and curves. Use the same colour for both the laid and couching threads, or choose contrasting threads.

◀ *This example uses perle thread for the laid threads and three strands of cotton embroidery thread for the couching. You can see that the spacing of the stitches and the angles of the points can be varied for different effects: sharp zigzags, steep or shallow points, and softer wavy lines.*

To work zigzag couching:

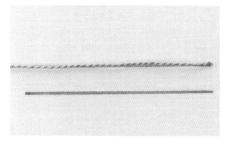

Step 1: Draw two parallel guidelines. Thread a needle with the laid thread and bring it up on the right-hand end of the top line. Lay the thread along the top line.

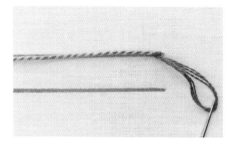

Step 2: Thread a second needle with the couching thread and bring it up through the fabric just below the laid thread, where it emerges from the fabric.

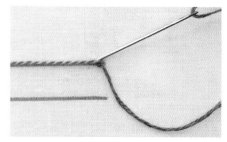

Step 3: Take the needle over the laid thread and back down through the fabric just above, forming a short vertical stitch; be sure not to pierce the laid thread.

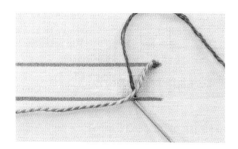

Step 4: Hold the laid thread along the lower line. Bring the needle with the couching thread up just above and a little to the left and take it over the thread to make another small vertical stitch.

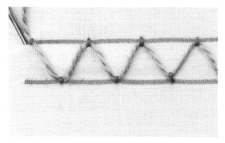

Step 5: Repeat the process along the line. When you reach the end, take the needle with the laid thread down through the fabric and fasten off on the wrong side.

TIP For a regular, even zigzag, mark the fabric with two parallel lines; for a more organic effect, you may prefer to work freestyle, without guidelines.

Tied Cross Stitch

This can be used as an isolated stitch or arranged in formal rows to create bands or an open filling. Any thread is suitable for this stitch but a firm, twisted type will give the best definition. The crosses can be any size you like.

Here the tied cross stitches are arranged in rows, with the 'legs' of the stitches touching. It creates an attractive trellis effect.

To work tied cross stitch:

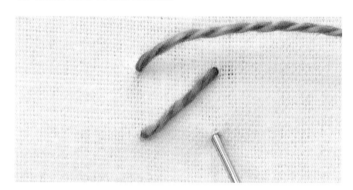

Step 1: Work a cross stitch in the usual way (see page 73).

Step 2: Bring the needle – with the same or a contrasting thread – up through the fabric to the left of the intersection.

Step 3: Take the needle over the centre and back through the fabric just to the right of the intersection.

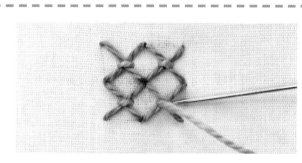

To create a trellis pattern: Arrange cross stitches with the ends of the 'legs' touching each other, then tie the intersections as described in steps 1–3.

Star Stitch

There are several variations of star stitch, some of them particularly suited to canvaswork and counted-thread embroidery rather than freestyle embroidery. This version – also known as star filling stitch when worked in multiples as an open filling – is a freestyle stitch suited to various fabrics; it can be worked in a single colour or in two or three colours, used singly or in rows, or scattered, to suit the design.

◀ *Scattered over an area, this stitch allows some colour variation: two shades for the points of the star and another colour for the tying cross stitch at the centre of each.*

To work star stitch:

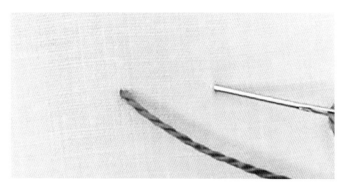

Step 1: Make a horizontal straight stitch of any length you like.

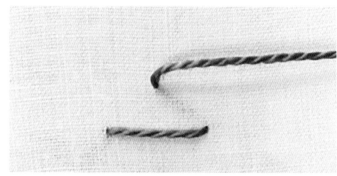

Step 2: Add a vertical stitch of the same length, crossing the first stitch and creating an upright cross.

Step 3: Now, with the same or a contrast thread, stitch a cross stitch (see page 73) on top, with each of the two diagonal stitches being the same length as the previous stitches.

Step 4: With the same thread or a different colour, make a smaller cross stitch, anchoring the centre of the star.

Thorn Stitch

With an appearance similar to a line of fern stitches (see page 69), this is a couched stitch that can be worked in a single colour or with two contrasting threads. Use it to depict ferns, grasses and spiked stems.

Soft cotton is used for the straight foundation stitch, with three strands of six-stranded cotton for the couching stitches that form the thorns. You can see from this example that thorn stitch is good for foliage and other plant forms.

To work thorn stitch:

Step 1: Make a long, straight stitch that will form the stem; keep this loose.

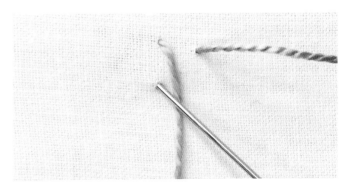

Step 2: Using a second thread, work a diagonal stitch across the long thread.

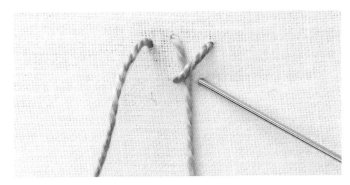

Step 3: Work a second diagonal stitch, crossing the long thread from the other side and also crossing the previous stitch.

Step 4: Continue working pairs of diagonal stitches at intervals, crossing over the laid thread and tying it to the fabric. Because the stitch is loose, you can manipulate it into a shallow curve, if you wish.

Romanian Stitch

An excellent filling stitch for small- to medium-sized shapes, this is a good alternative to Bokhara couching (see page 120). The laid threads should be close together, covering the fabric. This is one of the stitches that belongs in several different categories, as it can be regarded as a filling stitch or used to form a band or border.

Three strands of cotton embroidery thread give good coverage on a medium-sized shape like these carrots.

To work Romanian stitch:

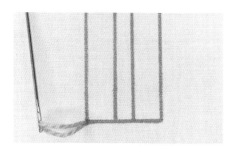

Step 1: Draw the shape to be filled; draw two central lines as a guide for the couching stitches. Bring the needle up through the fabric at the left, on the outline.

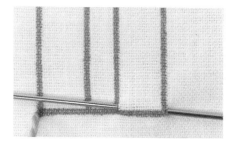

Step 2: Insert the needle back into the fabric on the opposite side of the outline, then bring it out on the right-hand central line.

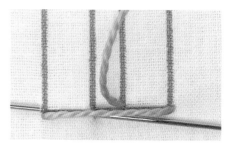

Step 3: Before pulling the thread through completely, work the couching stitch by bringing the needle over the laid thread and inserting it back in through the left-hand central line.

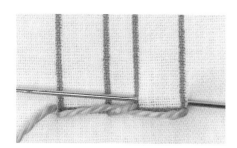

Step 4: Repeat the process, inserting the needle on the right and bringing it out again on the right-hand central line.

Step 5: Take the needle over the thread, insert it into the left-hand central line and bring it out on the left-hand side of the outline.

Step 6: Continue laying threads in this way, from left to right, working upwards and tying them with a short couching stitch each time.

Colcha Stitch

Originating in New Mexico, this attractive filling stitch is quick to work, so you can cover a large shape easily. The name comes from embroidered woollen hangings or bedcovers – called colchas – that were stitched using brightly coloured wools. It is a good alternative to Romanian stitch (see page 118).

The choice of a variegated thread helps to show the construction of the stitch quite clearly. Instead of being worked diagonally, the long stitches are worked horizontally across the shape.

To work colcha stitch:

Step 1: Draw the shape to be filled. Thread a needle with two lengths of thread. Make a long stitch across the centre of the shape. Traditionally, the laid stitches are placed diagonally.

Step 2: Couch the long stitch down at regular intervals with short diagonal stitches.

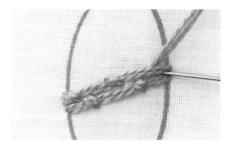

Step 3: Make another long stitch close to the previous one and tie it down in the same way, staggering the small couching stitches.

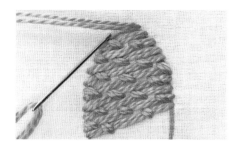

Step 4: Continue laying threads in this way, working upwards and tying them with short couching stitches.

Step 5: When one half of the shape has been filled, turn the work and fill the other half.

TIP Traditionally, the laid stitches are worked diagonally in colcha stitch – but it works just as well with stitches lying in any direction you choose.

Bokhara Couching

This solid filling stitch is idea for filling areas of any size or shape and uses the same thread for both the laid and the couching stitches. It has its origins in central Asia, notably Afghanistan and Uzbekistan, where it was used for bridal hangings and horse blankets.

◄ *This stitch is suitable for filling shapes with fairly irregular outlines and produces an effect like closely woven fabric. Here, a variegated perle thread is used effectively.*

To work Bokhara couching:

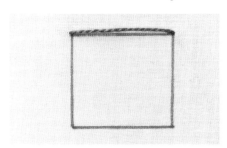

Step 1: Draw the shape to be filled; the lines will be covered by the stitches. Bring the needle up at the top left and take it across to the opposite side, forming a long stitch.

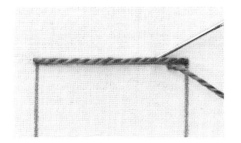

Step 2: Bring the needle up just along from the right-hand edge, then take it over the laid thread and down on the other side and very slightly to the left, creating a small, slanted couching stitch.

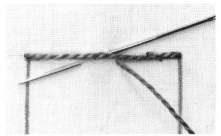

Step 3: Bring the needle out a little to the left and below the laid thread, then take it over the thread and back into the fabric. Bring the tip of the needle back out in position to create the next stitch.

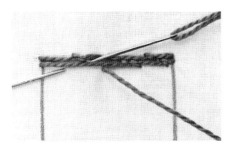

Step 4: Make another laid thread, close to the first, and couch this in the same way, positioning the couching stitches between those on the previous row.

Step 5: Continue filling the shape, staggering the couching stitches on each row.

TIP **Keep the laid stitches fairly loose to avoid puckering the fabric.**

Satin Stitch Couching

In this method, the laid thread is completely covered by the couching thread, producing a solid raised line like a cord. Use it for borders, outlines and monograms, plant stems in raised floral designs, and other applications that require a raised line. You can use multiple laid threads, depending on the effect you wish to achieve.

This scroll design, worked in three strands of six-stranded cotton embroidery thread, features lines of varying thicknesses.

To work satin stitch couching:

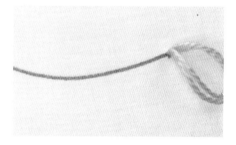

Step 1: Bring out the needle and laid threads at the start of the line to be covered.

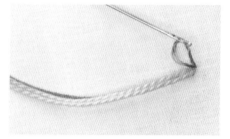

Step 2: Lay the threads along the line, guiding them with the fingers of your non-dominant hand. Bring out the couching thread at the beginning of the line.

Step 3: Work satin stitch (see page 103) over the laid threads, completely enclosing them. The satin stitches should be close together.

To work satin stitch couching:

Step 1: Simply add more threads; you can do this at any point on the line, prior to working the satin stitch embroidery.

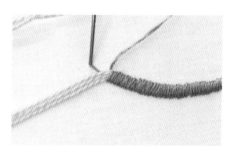

Step 2: At the end of the line, take all the laid thread ends through the fabric to the wrong side and secure them neatly.

Step 3: Cover the exposed laid threads with satin stitch, then take the couching thread to the wrong side and fasten off.

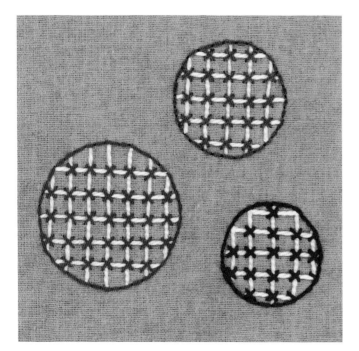

Jacobean Couching

In Jacobean embroidery, this attractive lattice stitch was often used to fill in large flower centres – but it has many other potential applications. Work it in a single colour, or with two contrasting threads, and use it to fill any fairly regular shape.

◄ *A simple shape such as a circle is easy to fill with this couched lattice pattern. Here, the laid threads are perle cotton and the couching stitches – the small crosses – are three strands of six-stranded cotton embroidery thread.*

To work Jacobean couching:

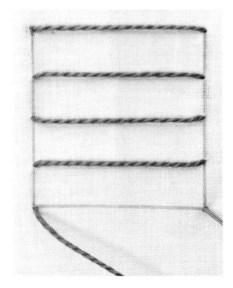

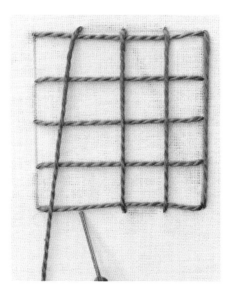

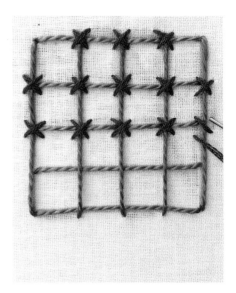

Step 1: Work long horizontal stitches, evenly spaced, across the area to be filled.

Step 2: Now work vertical stitches, at right angles to the horizontal stitches, to form a foundation grid.

Step 3: Where the laid threads intersect, work a small cross stitch (see page 73) to anchor the threads to the fabric.

Burden Stitch

This open filling stitch, originally a tapestry stitch dating from medieval times, is named after Mary Burden, a relative of William Morris, who popularised it as a surface embroidery stitch when teaching at the Royal School of Needlework in the 1870s. It can be used as a dense filling by positioning the vertical stitches close together or as a more open filling by spacing the stitches, allowing the background fabric to show through.

Satin thread is a good choice for the laid threads, providing an attractive sheen. A variegated six-stranded embroidery cotton creates is used for the couching.

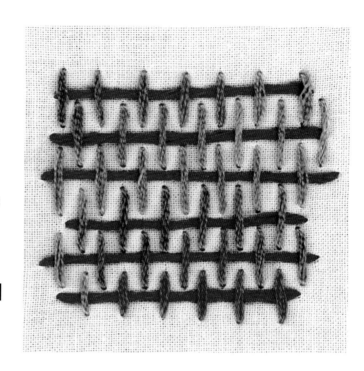

To work Burden stitch:

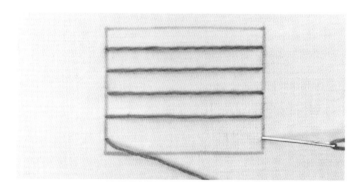

Step 1: Work long horizontal stitches across the whole width of the shape to be filled.

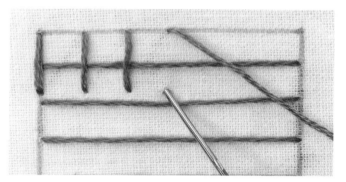

Step 2: With the same or a contrasting thread, work a series of upright straight stitches, evenly spaced, across the top row. Position the lower end of each stitch just above the horizontal thread below.

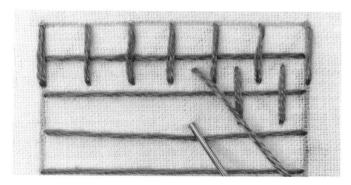

Step 3: Now work a series of upright stitches across the next horizontal thread, positioning them halfway between the ones in the row above.

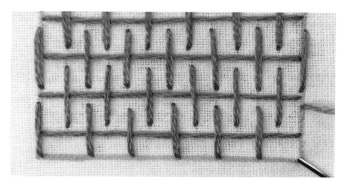

Step 4: Continue in this way, working across each horizontal thread in turn and offsetting stitches to resemble an open basketweave or brick pattern.

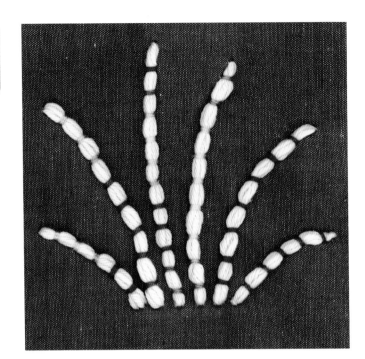

Bunched Couching

Producing a thickly textured line, straight or curved, this is an easy stitch to work and useful when you want to create a really chunky effect.

< *Five lengths of soft cotton embroidery thread are tied down with six-stranded embroidery cotton in a variegated shade. The effect is of a thick, rope-like cord.*

To work bunched couching:

Step 1: Bring the laid threads up at one end of the line (use several). If you are right-handed, it is easiest to start at the right; if you are left-handed, start at the left.

Step 2: Thread a second needle with a finer thread and bring it up a short distance from the start of the line, close to one side of the laid threads.

Step 3: Take the needle over the threads and back into the fabric on the other side, close to where it emerged.

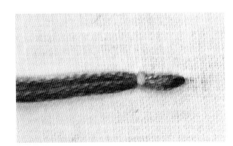

Step 4: Pull the thread tight, to hold the laid threads in place, but try not to pucker the fabric.

Step 5: Repeat the process, tying down the laid threads at intervals. At the end of the line, take all the threads to the wrong side and secure them.

TIP Thick embroidery can easily distort fabric and requires a robust support such as a heavy linen. It's also a good idea to stretch the ground fabric while stitching.

Couched Filling

This can be used to fill a simple geometric shaped area, especially where you wish to use a particularly thick thread or one that is too precious to be used for stitching.

This example shows that couched filling is equally effective worked either vertically or horizontally and can be combined with other stitches – in this case, satin stitch – for adding details.

To work couched filling:

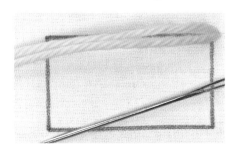

Step 1: Bring the laid thread up at the top of the shape to be filled, in the top right corner. Here, there are two laid threads: two lengths of soft cotton.

Step 2: Lay the threads flat along the top of the shape. Thread a second needle with the couching thread and bring it up through the fabric just below the point where the laid threads emerge.

Step 3: Take the needle over the threads and into the fabric immediately above, then bring the needle back out beneath the threads a little distance to the left.

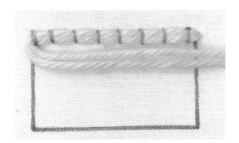

Step 4: Continue along the line, couching the laid threads at intervals. When you reach the top left corner, turn the threads, folding them back on themselves, and lay them below the first line.

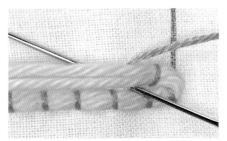

Step 5: You may find it easier to complete the next row if you turn the work. Couch the threads, positioning the couching stitches halfway between those of the previous row.

Step 6: At the end of the last line, take the needle with the laid threads through to the wrong side and fasten off.

Laid Satin Stitch

This technique starts with satin stitch and employs long couching stitches in the same or a contrasting colour to hold down the threads. It creates a dense filling suitable for most shapes and fairly large areas. Satin stitch alone is not suitable for covering medium or large areas, but this version means that long satin stitches are tied to the fabric, producing a neat result and helping to prevent snagging.

Using three strands of six-stranded embroidery cotton throughout, and subtle contrasts of colour, the laid threads provide a dense coverage and the couching threads form decorative detailing.

To work laid satin stitch:

Step 1: Fill the design area with satin stitch (see page 103), making sure that the stitches lie close together to provide good coverage.

Step 2: Using the same or a contrasting thread, work a straight stitch across the satin stitch, so that the couching stitch is at right angles to the laid threads.

Step 3: Now work small tying stitches across the couching thread, at regular intervals.

Step 4: Work further couching threads, keeping them regularly spaced.

Laidwork Trellis

A grid of diagonal stitches creates a trellis design laid over a satin-stitch foundation. Tiny crosses tie down the laid threads, adding intricate detailing.

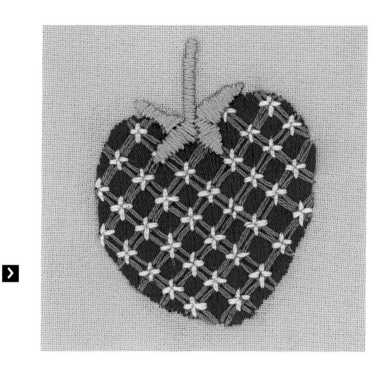

This strawberry shape has been filled with satin stitch in red, then overlaid with pairs of long stitches forming a diagonal trellis. Tied stitches, in yellow, suggest strawberry seeds. The stalk and leaf are worked in padded satin stitch (see page 104).

To work laidwork trellis:

Step 1: Fill the shape with satin stitches, arranging them close together for maximum coverage.

Step 2: Using a contrasting thread, work long stitches in pairs across the shape, with even spaces in between.

Step 3: Work further pairs, crossing the first set at right angles. Maintain a similar spacing between the pairs of threads.

Step 4: Tie down the laid threads by working four small stitches into the centre of the intersection. Work each cross in the same order: top to centre, left to centre, bottom to centre, then right to centre.

Step 5: When working the small crosses, be sure to insert the needle between the laid threads, taking care not to split them.

Couched Circle

This circular motif can be made in any size and is useful for all kinds of applications, particularly flower centres and wheels, as well as for creating decorative patterns. It can make a useful alternative to a woven wheel (see page 82) or a whipped wheel (see page 83).

◁ *Soft cotton embroidery thread has been used for the three larger circles and perle cotton for the three smaller ones, all couched with three strands of six-stranded embroidery cotton.*

To work couched circle:

Step 1: Draw a circle on the fabric; the lines will be covered by the stitches. Bring the laid thread up in the centre of the circle.

Step 2: Bring the couching thread up alongside the laid thread.

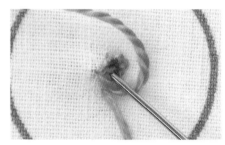

Step 3: Start to coil the laid thread around the central point and tie it down with a few small stitches worked across the thread.

Step 4: Lay the thicker thread in a smooth spiral, couching it down at regular intervals.

Step 5: When the shape has been filled and the drawn line covered, take both threads down through the fabric close to the circumference of the circle and fasten off on the wrong side.

Battlement Couching

Battlement couching, used extensively in Jacobean crewel work, would originally have been worked using woollen threads. The square grid is built up in layers and creates a three-dimensional effect.

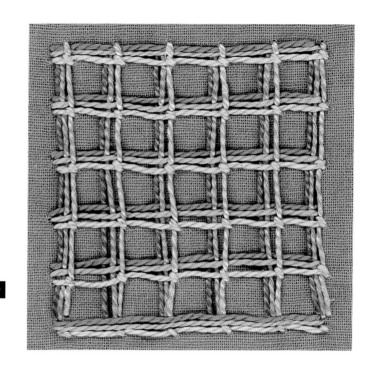

Using perle cotton (rather than the stranded cotton shown in the step-by-step photos below) in three close shades of blue produces a subtle shaded effect with a three-dimensional quality.

To work battlement couching:

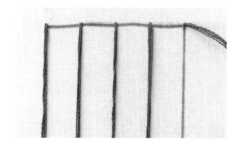

Step 1: Start with evenly spaced vertical straight stitches across the width of the shape to be filled.

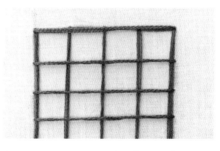

Step 2: Now work horizontal straight stitches across the verticals, to create a grid.

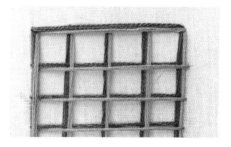

Step 3: With a second colour, work a second grid on top of the first, placing upright stitches to the right of the first set of verticals and horizontal stitches just below the horizontals.

Step 4: With a third colour, make another grid, once again offsetting the stitches, as in step 3.

Step 5: Using the same colour (though a contrasting thread has been used here, for clarity), secure each intersection of the third grid with a small diagonal stitch.

TIP You could work a fourth layer using an additional colour; in this case, do not work the tying stitches in step 3, but do this in step 4 with the colour used for the fourth grid.

Couched Beading

This method allows you to apply rows of beads in lines or as a filling within a shape and is quicker than stitching beads in place individually. You will need to use a fine needle with an eye that will accommodate the beading thread while at the same time being thin enough to pass through the hole in the centre of each bead.

◀ *Small glass beads – known as rocailles – are used here to create simple flower shapes.*

To work couched beading:

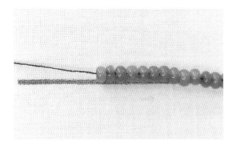

Step 1: Using a strong thread, bring the beading needle up through the fabric at one end of the design line. Thread on a number of beads and lay them along the line.

Step 2: Thread a second needle with thread to match the fabric (a contrasting colour is shown here for clarity). Bring the needle up close to the gap between the first and second beads.

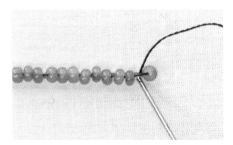

Step 3: Take the needle over the thread between the beads and into the fabric, making a tiny stitch that will couch the beading thread in place.

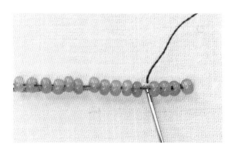

Step 4: Bring the needle up again a few beads along the line and make another small couching stitch.

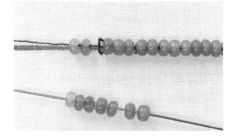

Step 5: Repeat the process working along the line, adding more beads as necessary.

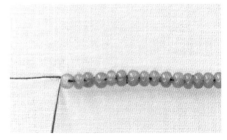

Step 6: At the end of the line, take the beading thread down into the fabric and secure it on the wrong side; do the same with the couching thread.

Shisha Stitch

Shisha is embroidery using mirrors and has its origins across Asia, particularly in India and Pakistan. It is sometimes called Indian mirror stitch. Shisha mirrors are available in various sizes. As the edges will be covered with thread once stitched in place, bear in mind that the mirror will appear slightly smaller. Any thread can be used, but stranded embroidery thread is easiest to work with and makes a firm edge.

Small round mirrors are held in place using three strands of embroidery cotton. You could also use other flat objects such as large sequins or coins, or even cut round discs from an old CD.

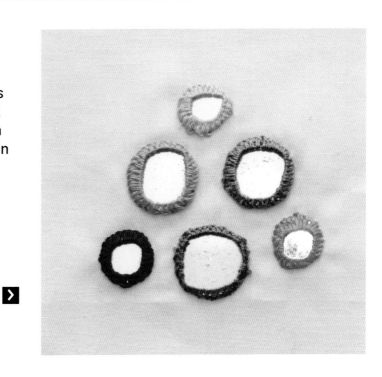

To work shisha stitch:

Step 1: Place the mirror on the fabric and hold it in place by working two horizontal stitches over the top. Take care when handling the mirror, as the roughly cut edges may be sharp.

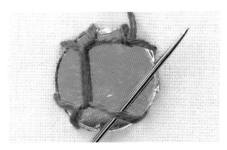

Step 2: Now work two vertical stitches, looping the thread around the horizontal threads. These four stitches are the holding stitches.

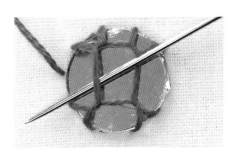

Step 3: Bring the needle up through the fabric at any point outside the edge of the mirror and take it over the holding thread. Pull through.

Step 4: Take the needle back into the fabric at the base of the same stitch and out again a small distance to the left, with the loop under the tip of the needle.

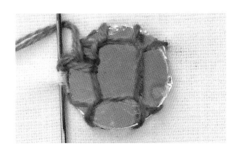

Step 5: Pull through, then take the needle over the holding thread again, then repeat step 4.

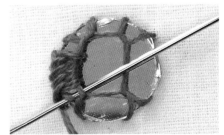

Step 6: Carry on in this way, all around the edge. When you come to one of the places where the holding threads intersect, take the needle over and under both.

Index

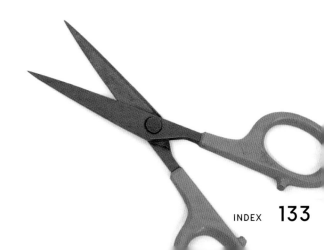

First published 2023 by

Guild of Master Craftsman Publications Ltd

Castle Place, 166 High Street, Lewes,

East Sussex BN7 1XU

ISBN 978-1-78494-650-0

The publishers and author can accept no legal responsibility for
any consequences arising from the application of information,
advice or instructions given in this publication.

A catalogue record for this book is available from the British Library.

Publisher **Jonathan Bailey**
Production **Jim Bulley**
Senior Project Editor **Virginia Brehaut**
Editor **Sarah Hoggett**
Design Manager **Robin Shields**
Designer **Rhiann Bull**

Colour origination by GMC Reprographics
Printed and bound in China

FSC
www.fsc.org
MIX
Paper | Supporting
responsible forestry
FSC® C020056

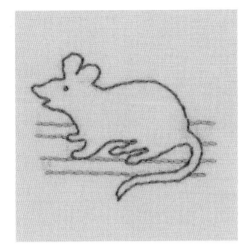

To place an order or to request
a catalogue, contact:

GMC Publications Ltd, Castle Place,
166 High Street, Lewes, East Sussex,
BN7 1XU, United Kingdom

Tel: +44 (0)1273 488005

www.gmcbooks.com